Apple Cider Vinegar
FOR HEALTH

100
Amazing and Unexpected Uses
for Apple Cider Vinegar

BRITT BRANDON, CFNS, CPT

FALL RIVER PRESS

New York

Dedication

For my amazing husband, Jimmy, and the loves of our lives: Lilly, Lonni, and JD. I am so thankful to have the wonderful family I have, and I want nothing more in this life than to have as many days as possible loving each of you!

FALL RIVER PRESS

New York

An Imprint of Sterling Publishing Co., Inc.
1166 Avenue of the Americas
New York, NY 10036

ISBN 978-1-4351-6633-2

For information about custom editions, special sales, and premium and corporate purchases, please contact Sterling Special Sales at 800-805-5489 or specialsales@sterlingpublishing.com.

Manufactured in China

2 4 6 8 10 9 7 5 3

sterlingpublishing.com

CONTENTS

INTRODUCTION

If you knew of a product that had been around for centuries, promoted by famous physicians and scholars, consumed by armies for boosting strength and maintaining the health of soldiers, utilized on battlegrounds for its healing properties, was even mentioned in the Bible, and had hundreds of health benefits that were well documented, would you want it? Of course you would! Imagine that this amazing all-natural product could be purchased right in your local grocery store for only a few dollars. This powerful potion *does* exist . . . it's called apple cider vinegar.

Every day, more and more people are turning to homeopathic, natural alternatives to the modern medicines that are prescribed for everything from a bee sting to the common cold. After all, many of these modern medicines deemed "safe" for over-the-counter sale come packed with harmful chemicals, possibly dangerous additives, and a host of possible side effects. Sure, they might work, but at what cost to your body?

Skip the pharmacy aisle and instead grab apple cider vinegar—an easy-to-find, simple-to-use, safe, all-natural, age-old solution that is well known for its reputation and effectiveness.

That's right—apple cider vinegar is a simplistic answer to so many of the minor and major woes we all experience. It's not a magical, expensive, or hard-to-get, celebrity-endorsed product that is advertised or skillfully marketed to the masses—it's an inexpensive product that is all-natural and has decades of support from both consumers and science.

Apple cider vinegar, or ACV, has been used for centuries by millions of people who attest to the amazing healing powers of this product. For less than the cost of a tube of toothpaste or a topical cream, ACV can be purchased, stored on your countertop or in your refrigerator, and used for everything from a bad-breath solution to a teeth-whitening agent, a sunburn soother to a varicose vein veiler, and (amazingly enough!) you can even drink the concoction on a daily basis to increase your metabolism and improve your body's immunity! Clearly, ACV has been a natural go-to solution for consumers that has stood the test of time *and* competition.

Modern technology has given companies new and improved ways to constantly bombard consumers with messages that try to convince you to purchase the "perfect" products that resolve issues you were previously unaware you even had (or were unaware you needed a medication for!). Meanwhile, ACV has stayed unassumingly on the condiment shelf of refrigerators, used primarily as a salad dressing ingredient.

It's time to harness the power of ACV in your life! Imagine replacing your expensive skin-care, hair-care, immunity-boosting, weight-loss products with an all-natural product that does it all . . . safely *and* effectively! By using ACV in combination with other everyday ingredients you already have around your house, you can save time, money, and sanity! Whether your goals are to improve your beauty regimen (to take care of your skin, hair, and nails), or improve the quality of your overall health, you'll find in this book a number of natural tips, tricks, and cures that will help you look and feel your best . . . naturally! Forgo the modern medicinal pills, potions, and creams that come with undesirable toxins, costs, and side effects, and find the answers to your problems with apple cider vinegar. Live a more natural life using a natural product with decades of positive support and statistics behind it, and opt for a "pennies on the dollar" approach to healing and helping yourself with apple cider vinegar. What have you got to lose?

APPLE CIDER VINEGAR'S MANY HEALTH BENEFITS

What Is Vinegar?

You can easily find apple cider vinegar in your local grocery store in its raw, organic, unfiltered state. This seemingly simplistic salad-dressing ingredient was perfectly packaged for purchase via a careful and concise production process few know anything about. Vinegar is the result of the natural sugars within carbohydrates (fruits, vegetables, or grains) being broken down by yeast and bacteria and turned into alcohol. The alcohol then undergoes a second fermentation process and voilà! Vinegar. The word "vinegar" is actually a literal French translation of the term for "sour wine," referring to the final product of the fermentation process.

While a wide variety of foods can be used to create this potent concoction, the nutritious and delicious apple is of course the main ingredient used to develop apple cider vinegar. Aside from apple cider vinegar, you can also find a wide variety of other vinegars, such as wine vinegars, rice vinegars, and coconut vinegars.

The Special Benefits of Apple Cider Vinegar

The beauty of the apple cider vinegar production process is that the amazing health benefits of apples remain intact. The key is to buy raw, unfiltered apple cider vinegar—that's the kind that's cloudy. Because of the careful process by which raw, undiluted apple cider vinegar is created, the essential nutrients that are so sought after remain intact and unadulterated. Apples are packed with vitamins and minerals, which give ACV its myriad health benefits. Here are the minerals present and their health benefits:

- **Potassium:** muscle contraction, nerve impulses, and energy production
- **Calcium:** important for bone health
- **Copper:** nerve functioning, bone maintenance, proper utilization of glucose

- **Iron:** transport of oxygen, blood health
- **Chromium:** regulating blood glucose
- **Magnesium:** synthesis of proteins, cellular energy production
- **Manganese:** formation and maintenance of bone, carbohydrate metabolism
- **Selenium:** antioxidant properties, fat metabolism
- **Sodium:** maintains proper fluid balance
- **Zinc:** promotes healing
- **Phosphorous:** proper cell functioning, strong bones

In addition to that impressive list of minerals, there are also a number of essential vitamins found in ACV:

- **Vitamin A:** eye health, powerful antioxidant
- **Vitamin C:** immune system functioning, powerful antioxidant
- **Vitamin E:** skin, nerve health; powerful antioxidant
- **Vitamin B_1:** nervous system functioning, digestive health, muscle health
- **Vitamin B_2:** promotes healthy skin, hair, and nails; aids in breakdown of proteins, carbs, and fats
- **Vitamin B_{12}:** red blood cell formation, proper nerve cell functioning
- **Vitamin B_6:** alleviates skin conditions and nerve damage, assists in utilization of proteins, carbs, and fats

Apples (and apple cider vinegar) also contain pectin, which has been shown to aid in digestion. That's how ACV is able to act as a cleansing agent and assist the colon in ridding the body of toxins and waste that have built up over time. The pectin in ACV forms a gel-like substance that makes debris easier to move in the digestive system so it gets carried away . . . naturally.

The "Mother" in Apple Cider Vinegar

If the long list of vitamins and minerals wasn't enough to impress, apple cider vinegar also contains the all-powerful "mother." "Mother" is the cobweb-like or sediment-like substance that can be seen floating in the *unfiltered* varieties of ACV. The mother contains the concentrated bacteria and enzymes that give ACV the antifungal, antiviral, and antibacterial healing powers for which it has become so famous. While some people may be caught off-guard by the sediment in their ACV bottles, this element is the result of the specific processing that retains the nutrients and enzymes of the apples throughout the fermentation process that provides the healing powers unique to ACV.

Are ACV Supplements Just as Beneficial?

You can also find ACV in supplement form in the vitamin aisle at your local pharmacy. While the supplement companies who produce this product claim that the benefits are the same as using ACV in its natural state, there is little research corroborating that. The truth is that while supplement manufacturers claim the potency of their products to be true, there is no real way of knowing what each tablet contains, how it's made, or the safety of consuming it. (Unlike medicines, the U.S. Food and Drug Administration doesn't regulate supplements.)

On the contrary, liquid ACV is produced by reputable companies who have been in the business of ACV production for years and are fervent advocates of their product's safety and effectiveness. While it may seem easier to swallow a tablet, the dangers of the supplement version are proven; in one specific case, a consumer suffered serious esophageal damage when an apple cider vinegar tablet became stuck in her throat. The acidic foundation of ACV makes a supplement potentially harmful. When you dilute the liquid form, you're eliminating that hazard.

A Few Caveats

After reading about the amazing benefits of apple cider vinegar, you're probably eager to start using it. But, before you rush out to grab this miracle product, there are a few things to consider.

- **Talk with your doctor first.** Before you begin using any new health product or start a new health regimen, consult your physician to ensure that there are no risks of that product interfering with current medications, agitating current illnesses, or posing a health risk in any way.

- **Always dilute it.** Because of its high acidity, ACV should never be consumed straight or without dilution to avoid damage to tooth enamel and tissues within the mouth, esophagus, and stomach.
- **Diabetics, take note!** Research suggests that chromium can alter insulin levels. People with diabetes should seek approval from their physician prior to using ACV.
- **Check bone density.** Those who suffer from osteoporosis or already experience low potassium levels should also consult their physicians prior to consuming ACV to ensure that the health benefits of an ACV regimen outweigh any risks.
- **Be aware of allergies.** Since ACV is an apple-based product, people with apple allergies should seek approval from their physician prior to using ACV.

While most people will never experience any type of harmful side effects by using recommended amounts of ACV, it is important to know the risks . . . and recognize that there are still far fewer than many of the seemingly harmless products and medications on the market today.

Why Haven't I Heard of This Before?!

If you've never heard of apple cider vinegar being used for home remedies, you're not alone. ACV is not a heavily promoted product. There are no major marketing strategies pushing the public to run out to purchase bottles of ACV to cure what ails them. Instead, products that contain potentially harmful elements, produce undesirable side effects, or cost an exorbitant amount of money grace the magazine pages, radio ads, and television commercials we see and hear every day. Competing with these heavily marketed products, though, ACV's all-natural cure-all reputation has been enough to allow this product to stay available, remain inexpensive, and actually grow in popularity over the years.

It's time for you to join the millions of people who have experienced the power and are enjoying the benefits of apple cider vinegar, and see for yourself how much you can change your life . . . one drop of ACV at a time!

Part 1

HEALTH

Chapter 1: **NUTRITION**

Every year, consumers spend billions of dollars on health products that focus on diet. Between products promising to help you lose weight and build muscle, vitamin supplements to remedy deficiencies and improve system functioning, and products designed to relieve stomach troubles, this is a huge industry that pumps out products packed with, well, who knows what. You never truly know what is really in your daily vitamins, what those cryptic ingredients are in the lengthy list on the back of your appetite suppressant, or what makes the active ingredient in your anticonstipation medicine so "active." We trustingly hand over hard-earned money for a product that may not even deliver what it promises, and could actually cause more harm than good. If you're looking to improve your diet, enrich your body with quality nutrition, reverse deficiencies, and resolve stomach issues, you need to look no further than apple cider vinegar.

With rich amounts of vitamins like vitamin C, B vitamins, vitamin A, and vitamin E, along with essential minerals like iron, magnesium, potassium, and calcium, ACV is your one-stop shop for maintaining sufficient amounts of the nutrients you need to keep your body and mind running as they should. But the benefits provided by ACV don't stop there! With pectin, a naturally occurring element in apples that acts as a fibrous gel when it's introduced to your digestive enzymes, and a variety of antioxidants that work to prevent illness and protect cell health, ACV goes above and beyond the average vitamin supplement.

One of the most exciting aspects of using apple cider vinegar to improve your health is that you don't have to worry about side effects from dangerous chemical additions as with so many over-the-counter health products. Because the active ingredients and nutritional benefits of ACV are the results of simple methods designed to retain the natural elements of the apples used to create the vinegar, there is no need to add anything. Naturally, you can achieve your goals of maximizing your metabolic functioning, satisfying your body's needs for specific vitamins, and minimizing your need for medications designed to help with digestion or aid in suppressing appetite.

1 Improve Weight Loss

Whether it's a New Year's resolution, an upcoming wedding, preparation for bikini season, or one of so many reasons millions choose to start weight-loss programs, people spend billions of dollars every year to lose weight. Yet many of the diet pills, potions, and plans fail to deliver, leaving those who paid out feeling duped . . . and still wanting to lose those annoying pounds. The plan with the highest success rate for losing weight and maintaining weight loss involves a quality, clean diet and exercise regimen, and apple cider vinegar can help too!

Including ACV in your weight-loss plan is easy to do and really effective.

TO MAKE A DAILY DOSE, COMBINE:

1 cup water

1 tablespoon ACV

1 tablespoon lemon juice

Drink the concoction up to five times daily prior to meals to enjoy the many health benefits that can aid in weight loss.

Most people cite the following four obstacles in achieving and maintaining weight loss:

1. Not being able to control hunger/cravings

2. Having an insatiable appetite

3. Lack of energy

4. A slow metabolism

The naturally occurring elements in ACV can help you overcome each one of those challenges. See entries 2 and 3 for more on how to use ACV for weight-loss success.

2 Speed Up Metabolism

A fast metabolism is something that only "skinny" people have, right? Wrong! Genetics do play a very important role in metabolism, but *any* person can improve his or her rate of metabolism naturally. Try this invigorating ACV recipe:

TO MAKE A DRINK, COMBINE:

1 cup green tea

2 tablespoons ACV

1 tablespoon lemon juice

1 teaspoon ground cayenne pepper

To use, drink this metabolism-boosting tonic 30 minutes before every meal.

The combination of caffeinated green tea, internal-temperature-raising cayenne pepper, and multiple vitamins and minerals in lemon juice and ACV promotes proper metabolic functioning, improves fat burning, and increases energy levels.

Along with this drink, try these simple lifestyle changes to boost your metabolic rates in a matter of weeks:

- Implement a strength-training routine designed to increase fat-burning muscle mass
- Eat smaller meals more frequently throughout the day
- Incorporate 30-minute bouts of cardiovascular exercise 4–6 days per week

3 Suppress Your Appetite

Ever been on a diet, peering into your refrigerator, looking for *something* to stop your stomach from growling? Even though you've been able to stick to your diet, eat clean foods, and drink loads of water, you still find yourself hungry and with a seemingly insatiable appetite that is sure to lead to diet derailment in no time. Rather than give in to temptation or suffer through the feelings of starvation and deprivation, choose the healthy alternative: apple cider vinegar.

TO MAKE A DRINK, COMBINE:

2 cups water

1 tablespoon ACV

To use, stir well, and sip throughout the day.

The enzymes and acetic acid in ACV normalizes the acid levels (pH levels) of your stomach, reducing hunger pains and cravings, and resulting in a reduced appetite. There are other theories about why ACV helps regulate appetite, too. One theory is that the acetic acid in ACV reduces the glycemic index of foods, which slows the rate that sugars are released into the blood stream, prolonging the feeling of satiety after a meal and reducing cravings. Another theory is that the pectin in ACV mixes with water/liquid and expands, leading to a decrease in appetite. Regardless of *how* it works, it does! The best part about this tonic is that it's easy to make, and very portable . . . making it a simple option to reach for instead of a food you'd eat and regret later.

Place a sticky note or index card on your fridge or cabinet where your favorite craving foods are stored reminding you of your ACV appetite-suppressing option. This way, you see the reminder every time you reach for foods that aren't diet-friendly.

④ Aid Fasting

Fasting is one of the age-old, tried-and-true remedies for cleansing the body of toxins and allowing yourself a "break" from a diet of excess. Whether the excess is in the form of alcohol, fattening foods, or an overall unhealthy way of eating and drinking, a simple and easy fast that includes ACV will provide a "clean slate" from which you can start a new way of eating clean and living better in just a matter of days. While some people look forward to a fast because of the inherent promise that they'll feel rejuvenated, refreshed, and renewed, many others dread the thought of a fast, thinking only of the feelings of starvation. If you're hesitant to even entertain the idea, consider ACV "fasting." It is different from so many other options because you can still eat foods during the fast.

Paul C. Bragg was the "pioneer" manufacturer and promoter of apple cider vinegar in its purest form. He used his product for maintaining health and vitality and resisting illness throughout his life. He recommended a fast using his own product (Bragg's unfiltered, organic ACV) in a tonic designed to flush the system of waste, while also maintaining a strict diet of whole foods including fruits, vegetables, nuts, and seeds. By flushing the system with fiber-rich ACV, fruits, and vegetables, the body's systems are better able to get rid of built-up waste products. During this cleanse, the body can naturally adjust to a new diet of healthy whole foods intended to keep the body free of waste by "keeping things moving."

TO MAKE BRAGG'S TONIC, COMBINE:

1   cup water

1   tablespoon ACV (or start with ½ tablespoon and build up to 1 tablespoon)

½ tablespoon lemon juice

Consume 3–5 times per day for 7–10 days.

⑤ Detoxify Your Liver

Few people know what the liver actually does. The liver is an organ that secretes bile in order to aid in effective digestion, but its duties go far beyond that! The liver also protects and promotes one's vitality by:

- Filtering toxins and waste products in the blood
- Producing energy by manufacturing essential proteins and storing carbohydrates and other essential nutrients
- Properly metabolizing fats

Keeping the liver free of dangerous toxins that compromise its ability to function properly is an essential step in maintaining overall health and wellness.

You can safeguard the optimal functioning of your liver by consuming a diet and living a lifestyle that presents the liver with a lighter workload:

- Eat a clean diet that includes whole foods like fruits, vegetables, nuts, and seeds
- Drink minimal alcohol

- Drink lots of clear fluids (preferably water)
- Avoid toxic substances like nicotine and drugs (prescription and otherwise)

Apple cider vinegar makes for the perfect partner in liver detoxification by contributing its variety of vitamins, minerals, and enzymes to maintain a healthy pH balance.

TO MAKE A LIVER-CLEANSING DRINK, COMBINE:

1   cup water

1–2   teaspoons ACV

½ teaspoon raw honey

Drink three times a day.

6 Flush Your Gallbladder

The gallbladder is an organ that aids the body's systems in flushing out toxins and waste by producing the bile the liver secretes. Hand-in-hand with the liver, the gallbladder plays an important part in maintaining a proper pH balance of the body, while also removing health-harming toxins. Maintaining the health of this organ is, obviously, essential in maintaining optimal health, which is why you should consider a flush of the gallbladder with apple cider vinegar. By performing this gallbladder cleanse twice a year, you can help your gallbladder function as intended.

TO MAKE THIS CLEANSE, COMBINE:

1 cup water

½ tablespoon ACV

2 tablespoons apple juice (organic, unfiltered, not from concentrate)

Consume twice a year.

A cleanse like this can also help you avoid gallstones, which are pebble-like deposits that form inside the organ. Some people with gallstones have no symptoms, while others experience excruciating pain. Gallstones are thought to be caused by one of these situations:

1. When the gallbladder's bile is not effective enough to dissolve the liver's cholesterol production, the excess cholesterol crystalizes and creates gallstones.

2. When the bile contains too much bilirubin (the result of the chemical breakdown of red blood cells).

3. A condition known as cirrhosis of the liver, causing the liver to produce excessive amounts of bilirubin.

4. The gallbladder's ability to empty bile correctly is compromised, leading to bile becoming concentrated and forming the gallstones.

Gallstones can block the passage of bile and cause extreme pain when leaving the gallbladder—use the ACV cleanse to help avoid them.

7 Reduce Flatulence

There are few things as embarrassing as excessive flatulence. Embarrassing, uncomfortable, and difficult to deal with, excessive gas and flatulence is a condition for which the number of over-the-counter remedies run in the thousands. Chemically manufactured pills and drinks that promise to reduce the incidence of gas may be effective, but they often include countless chemicals and ingredients you can't pronounce.

While myriad medical conditions can cause excessive gas, most people who experience sporadic bouts of bloating and gas can point to unhealthy foods as the cause. Unhealthy diets wreak havoc on the digestive system, leaving excessive gas in their wake. However, even those who eat clean diets full of fibrous roughage, such as cruciferous vegetables (broccoli, cauliflower, etc.), can suffer from excessive gas buildup and frequent flatulence.

No matter what causes gas, ACV can help alleviate it. By combining a diet of healthy whole foods that calm gas-producing conditions such as honey, fennel, ginger, flax, cinnamon, and pineapple with all-natural ACV tonics that treat gas, you can experience far less flatulence. The active acids and enzymes of ACV help to alleviate gas production and flatulence by negating the gas-producing elements and processes involved.

TO MAKE A TONIC TO TREAT GAS, COMBINE:

1 cup water

1 teaspoon honey

1 teaspoon peppermint extract

½ teaspoon cinnamon

1 tablespoon ACV

Drink daily.

8 Calm Heartburn

For the millions of heartburn sufferers, the number of remedies (both natural and medicinal) can be overwhelming. Pills, liquids, recommendations on what to do both pre- and post-meal—it's enough stress to give you, well, heartburn! Good news—forget all those options and instead grab apple cider vinegar, which has been used to treat heartburn for years. Opponents say there is little research to support the claim, but many people report that it works wonders. What do you have to lose? Give the all-natural option a try.

TO MAKE A DRINK, COMBINE:

1   cup water

1   teaspoon ACV

1   teaspoon honey

To use, drink every 30 minutes until heartburn subsides.

The true crux of the heartburn issue is the imbalance of acids in the stomach, potentially caused by one of these factors:

- The inability of your body to effectively break down fats

- A bad reaction resulting from a nutrient-poor diet
- A stomach that seems to battle foods more often than accepting them

The main component of apple cider vinegar that makes it so effective in treating heartburn is the acetic acid that results from the fermentation of the apples. While it seems surprising that you would treat heartburn by introducing acid, the naturally occurring acetic acid of ACV is far weaker than the hydrochloric acid produced by the stomach and actually acts as a buffer by helping to alleviate and prevent heartburn by bringing the acidic level in the stomach to a more normal level.

9 Ease Indigestion

While many people use the terms "heartburn" and "indigestion" interchangeably, they are actually two different conditions. Indigestion is defined as discomfort in the stomach associated with digesting food. Indigestion can be caused by a number of factors acting individually or combined, and it strikes people of both genders, all ages, and, surprisingly, even those who adhere to the strictest of healthy diets. Here are some common causes:

- Overeating
- Eating spicy or acidic foods
- Allergic reactions or intolerances to specific foods such as gluten, lactose, or excessively fatty or greasy foods

The underlying problem that leads to all cases of indigestion is inadequate stomach acid for digestion. Antacids are the common prescription for indigestion, yet they rarely cure it because they don't address the problem. By calming the stomach's acidic state naturally with a balancing acid (not an antacid), the stomach returns to a healthy pH balance.

When consuming ACV, you supplement the inadequate stomach acid with a less intense version— acetic acid. Safely, easily, and naturally, the acetic acid can help soothe the symptoms of indigestion.

TO MAKE A DRINK, COMBINE:

1   cup water

2–4   teaspoons ACV

To use, sip the concoction over a period of 20–30 minutes. You should feel relief of the indigestion symptoms. If the relief is taking longer than expected, or not working effectively enough, create the same concoction again, using twice as much ACV as in the first concoction (for example, if you used 2 teaspoons ACV in the first mixture, you can use up to 4 teaspoons in the second). Again, sip over a period of 20–30 minutes.

10 Soothe Stomachaches

Stomachaches can be caused by a number of disruptions that range from psychological stresses and poor lifestyle choices to bad habits and prolonged exposure to unhealthy irritants. You might experience acute stomachaches once in a while, or you might be plagued with less painful but longer-lasting versions. No matter why you get stomachaches, you can effectively minimize their severity, frequency, and duration by attacking the root of the problem, rather than treating the symptoms that result.

Ensuring that your digestive system, from your saliva to your colon, is running effectively, you can prevent stomachaches from occurring, and treat them once they strike. By regulating the pH balance of your entire digestive system, ACV begins fighting the causes of stomachaches. By fighting off bacteria, viruses, and possible irritants that could further exacerbate a stomachache, ACV is able to aid in relieving the body of possible illnesses or invaders that can cause or exacerbate uneasiness.

TO MAKE A DRINK, COMBINE:

1 cup water

1 tablespoon ACV

Sip the solution over a period of 30 minutes to experience relief from stomachaches.

11 Alleviate Morning Sickness

There are a million beautiful aspects of pregnancy that only a mother can truly understand. Between watching your belly grow and feeling the flutter of the first kick, the miracle of pregnancy is truly awe-inspiring and joyful. One downside of pregnancy, however, is the queasiness, nausea, or vomiting that many women encounter. Inaccurately referred to as "morning sickness," this uneasy feeling can actually strike at any time of day and can range from mild to severe.

Because there are different degrees in the severity of morning sickness, some choose to "ride it out" while others use prescription medications for relief. While each case of morning sickness is as unique as the sufferer, apple cider vinegar is a natural remedy that may aid in calming or curing morning sickness.

TO MAKE A MORNING SICKNESS RELIEF DRINK, COMBINE:

2 cups water

½–1 tablespoon ACV

¼" peeled portion of ginger

Sip the mixture over the course of an hour and experience relief.

ACV contains a multitude of vitamins and minerals that can improve the quality of a pregnancy by benefitting both mom and fetus, such as:

- Vitamins A, Bs, C, and E
- Minerals like potassium, magnesium, and iron
- Stomach-settling fiber and enzymes

These nutrients combine to help pregnant women:

- Regulate their body's pH balance
- Neutralize digestive enzymes, improving digestion
- Minimize bouts of constipation and diarrhea that can also contribute to morning sickness

12 Relieve Bouts of Constipation

There is no doubt that constipation is an unpleasant digestive condition to deal with. You have a constant feeling that you have to go, but can't. You remain hopefully tethered to your toilet, suffer from stomachaches and bad breath (bad breath is a common symptom of constipation!), plus that horrible gas and bloating! What's worse is that this situation can drag on for over a week. Those who are on a regular pooping schedule may feel the serious discomfort of constipation symptoms just a few hours past missing their regularly expected poop.

While a number of remedies are available in the medicine aisles of your favorite drugstore, many of them come packed with chemicals, dangerous side effects, or, ahem, *explosive* results that deliver far more pain than the original symptoms caused. If you prefer a more natural alternative to forcible forms of constipation relief, look no further than your trusty bottle of apple cider vinegar.

Packed with pectin, iron, acetic acid, and fiber, ACV relieves constipation by forming a goo-like fibrous supplement in the digestive system, helping the stool soften, form more appropriately, and move along. As a softer, fuller stool forms, many people are able to use the restroom successfully within an hour or two, naturally and without those extreme side effects.

TO FIND RELIEF IMMEDIATELY, SIMPLY COMBINE:

1   tablespoon ACV

1   cup water

Drink the concoction over the course of 30 minutes.

TO PREVENT THE SITUATION FROM OCCURRING AGAIN, TRY THIS COMBINATION OF TREATMENTS:

- Drink this mixture up to three times daily
- Drink plenty of additional water
- Abstain from caffeinated beverages
- Eat naturally fibrous whole foods like fruits, vegetables, nuts, and seeds

13 Overcome Diarrhea

Diarrhea always seems to occur at the most inopportune times. Whether you're safe at home or at a black-tie affair, though, there is never a good time to come down with this debilitating symptom. Diarrhea is referred to as a *symptom* and not a *condition* because diarrhea is the way the body deals with an unwanted element in the digestive system. Whether the irritant be a fried food that isn't being digested properly, a virus attempting to attack the immune system, or a more extreme case of parasites, diarrhea is the body's natural way of quickly purging the irritant from the body and safeguarding one's health and vitality.

Because diarrhea rids the body of the problematic irritant, over-the-counter diarrhea medications designed to stop you from going are not the right remedy. When you ingest a formulation designed to stop the diarrhea, it may seem great in the short term, but it actually allows the irritant trying to be purged from the body to instead fester in the digestive system for hours longer, wreaking havoc and possibly spreading to other previously unaffected organs. Medicinal remedies can also lead to unintentional constipation, which means you've just traded one uncomfortable problem for another.

The active ingredients in apple cider vinegar that assist in resolving diarrhea naturally are pectin, iron, and acetic acid. These three simple elements combine to form a fibrous gel that acts as a lubricant within the digestive system, while also adding bulk to the stool. What results is nothing short of a miracle cure! In as few as thirty minutes, ACV moves waste quickly through the system, but in a form that is far more comfortable than previously experienced.

TO MAKE A DRINK TO RESOLVE DIARRHEA, COMBINE:

1 cup warm water

1–2 tablespoons ACV

Drink the mixture over a period of 15 minutes. It is safe to consume this concoction repeatedly every hour until the diarrhea subsides.

14 Avoid Bacterial Cystitis

Bacterial cystitis is a medical term that is used interchangeably with the better-known term "urinary tract infection" or UTI. Cystitis is defined as an inflammation of the bladder, most commonly caused by bacteria. The alternative to the bacterial cause is interstitial cystitis (see next entry). The bacterial version of cystitis more commonly occurs in women, but it can also be experienced by men and children; women are particularly susceptible to the condition because of their shorter urethras, which are more easily exposed to harmful bacteria. The condition starts out feeling like a tingling sensation and can then become severe, with symptoms that cause the sufferer to feel the frequent urge to urinate, with or without urine being expelled, and can include pain and burning sensations experienced during urination. Because bacterial cystitis is a bacterial infection of the bladder, antibiotics are the normal course of treatment, but natural methods can be used to prevent and alleviate the condition.

Packed with valuable vitamins and minerals that assist in flushing the body of toxins such as the harmful bacteria that contribute to this uncomfortable condition, apple cider vinegar makes for the perfect preventive option in stopping bacterial cystitis before it starts. There are two ways to do this:

TO MAKE A DRINK, COMBINE:

1   cup water

1   tablespoon ACV

Drink daily. Many women report experiencing fewer incidences of bacterial cystitis than prior to starting an ACV regimen, and they experienced a reduced severity in symptoms when they consumed the concoction following the onset of the condition.

You can also try this bathing method:

COMBINE IN A BATHTUB:

1   cup ACV

Tub full of warm water

Soak for 30 minutes. This bath alleviates symptoms by killing bacteria in the urethra.

15 Limit Interstitial Cystitis

While bacterial cystitis is a commonly experienced bacterial infection that causes inflammation of the bladder, interstitial cystitis is a persistent condition characterized by inflammation of the submucosal and muscular layers of the bladder. Sometimes referred to as bladder pain syndrome, or BPS, interstitial cystitis is characterized by severe symptoms such as blood in the urine, intense pelvic pain, and the sudden urge to urinate (with or without urine being excreted) up to sixty times per day. The most daunting aspect of this condition is that it has no known cause and no known cure. Doctors are still stumped as to whether the condition is hereditary, a birth defect, due to vascular disease, or aggravated by allergies. With no known cure for the condition, many sufferers are forced to endure the pain without treatment, or in the most severe cases, have the bladder removed.

Some interstitial cystitis sufferers opt for preventive measures they can take at home. They carefully determine what physical, diet, or environmental factors contribute to their flare-ups of the condition. While there is no cure, interstitial cystitis has shown to improve with the limiting of certain foods and drinks like sodas, caffeinated beverages, and citrus fruits and drinks. In addition to limiting aggravating dietary elements, apple cider vinegar may help to calm the condition by:

- Supplying nutrients that assist the bladder in processing urine
- Minimizing the toxicity of the urine
- Detoxifying the blood and body fluids that play a part in the bladder's functioning

You can introduce ACV into your body through this simple, versatile tonic:

TO MAKE A DRINK, COMBINE:

1 cup water

1 tablespoon ACV

Consume the beverage over the course of 30 minutes, and continue to drink the same combination every hour until symptoms subside.

16 Increase Calcium Absorption

While most people assume they know the importance of calcium, few know the profound effects this essential mineral has on a number of systems in the body. The most well-known role of calcium is building and maintaining strong bones and teeth—and indeed, 99 percent of your body's calcium is stored in the bones and teeth. What few people know, though, is that this essential mineral is also valuable for:

- Cognition
- Proper nervous system functioning
- Maintaining muscle mass
- Preventing blood pressure issues

Without a doubt, when it comes to maintaining one's overall health, calcium is one of the most important minerals. With all of the calcium supplements and calcium-fortified products available, you may be under the impression that you're getting enough of this magical mineral in your diet—but you may be mistaken. While supplementing may help, a diet including calcium-rich foods—including apple cider vinegar!—is the best way to consume calcium.

Surprisingly enough, a better way to ensure you're actually absorbing the most calcium from your foods is to start an apple cider vinegar regimen that can contribute two essentials needed to maximize calcium absorption from the foods you eat every day: acetic acid and magnesium. The acetic acid that is found in ACV actually promotes the body's absorption of calcium by assisting in the breaking down of calcium-rich foods and aiding in their digestion. Calcium-rich foods like deep-green veggies contain compounds called oxalates that actually block calcium absorption. The acetic acid in ACV neutralizes these oxalates and makes the ingested calcium more easily absorbed. In addition to the acetic acid, ACV also contains magnesium, which aids in calcium absorption.

TO MAKE A DRINK THAT HELPS WITH CALCIUM ABSORPTION, COMBINE:

1   cup calcium-fortified orange juice

1   tablespoon ACV

Drink daily.

17 Minimize Iron Deficiency

Iron deficiency is defined as an inadequate supply of red blood cells, which leads to tissues being deprived of essential oxygen. Common symptoms are extreme fatigue and weakness. In addition to a short supply of red blood cells, the body's failure to produce enough red blood cells or excessive bleeding (even heavy menstrual flows can qualify as excessive bleeding) can be to blame. While some symptoms of iron deficiency (also known as iron-deficiency anemia or anemia) are mild enough that they can go unnoticed for a lengthy period of time, many anemia symptoms are powerful enough to change one's day-to-day life dramatically. When the body's ability to absorb and utilize enough iron is compromised, many of the body's systems are affected, and the result is as wide a variety of symptoms, such as:

- Fatigue
- Mood swings
- A compromised immune system

By taking an over-the-counter iron supplement, you can moderate iron deficiency, but by consuming ACV daily, you can assist in iron absorption and reduce the need for supplements on a regular basis.

TO MAKE AN IRON-BOOSTING DRINK, COMBINE:

2   cups water

2   tablespoons ACV

½ cup spinach

½ green apple, cored

Combine all ingredients in a blender and blend until thoroughly combined.

Drink daily.

18 Limit Potassium Deficiencies

Potassium is one of the miraculous minerals that doesn't get enough attention for how large a role it plays in maintaining proper functioning in the body. Potassium controls muscle growth, muscle contraction, nerve cell functioning, and protein synthesis, for starters. Few people know how to maximize potassium's benefits or ensure their body is getting enough. Potassium levels in the body fluctuate naturally, and are directly affected by your body's sodium levels. With water weight fluctuating unnaturally due to illness, nutrition, or lifestyle factors (menstruation, pregnancy, or menopause), you can find yourself dealing with bloating or dehydration, neither of which is comfortable or healthy.

The minerals, acetic acid, and enzymes contained in apple cider vinegar are effective in maintaining potassium levels in a healthy balance strong enough to avoid deficiencies.

TO MAKE A POTASSIUM-RICH DRINK, COMBINE IN A BLENDER:

1 cup almond milk

1 tablespoon ACV

1 banana

½ cup ice

Drink as a meal or snack one to three times per week.

Hypokalemia is the term for potassium deficiency. It takes extreme measures, or a combination of factors, to have potassium levels dip low enough to qualify as dangerous. In terms of environmental factors, exposure to prolonged heat or extensive bouts of physical exertion (physical labor outdoors or exercise) can result in excessive sweating; these situations can lead to a fluctuation in fluid levels and sodium balance, directly affecting the potassium levels in the body. Health conditions that require certain medications such as diuretics or treatments such as antibiotics can also deplete potassium levels.

19 Avoid Vitamin C Deficiencies

When your body is in good overall health, each of your body's systems can function at its full capability. Most people suffer from ailments when their immune system is compromised. Whether it's a common cold, vitamin or mineral deficiency, or more serious health condition, you become susceptible to a number of other health risks if your immune system is not working properly. Even prescriptions and over-the-counter medications can compromise the immune system's ability to fight disruptions in the body's natural balances of minerals, fluids, and bacteria; this situation is commonly seen when antibiotics eliminate the illness intended but promote the growth of harmful bacteria that results in yeast infections. Without a doubt, when the body's systems are operating more effectively, and synergistically, your immune system benefits greatly!

You know now that apple cider vinegar provides essential vitamins, minerals, and enzymes. It also has antiviral and antibacterial properties that combine to assist the immune system in fighting illnesses while also ensuring the body functions at optimal levels. This optimal functioning includes absorbing essential dietary nutrients and utilizing them more effectively. Apple cider vinegar contains vitamin C and helps you absorb it more efficiently, too. By drinking ACV, you can kick-start a beneficial cycle that improves the body's immunity, enables the body to better absorb the vitamin, improving the immunity, and so on.

TO MAKE A DAILY VITAMIN C–BOOSTING DRINK, COMBINE:

- 1 cup organic apple juice (not from concentrate)
- 1 frozen banana
- 1 cup frozen strawberries
- 1 teaspoon cinnamon
- 1 tablespoon ACV

Combine all ingredients in a blender and blend until desired consistency is achieved. Enjoy once daily.

20 Avoid B-Vitamin Deficiencies

B vitamins are responsible for ensuring the proper functioning of a surprising number of systems. B vitamins play an important part in the body's overall health, including:

- Maintaining positive mindset (vitamin B deficiencies are associated with depression)
- Promoting proper protein synthesis
- Nourishing nerve cells
- Supplying the essential elements for DNA synthesis

Surprisingly enough, most people are unaware of how to include more B-vitamin-rich foods in their diet to avoid suffering from a B-vitamin deficiency. Foods such as nuts, seeds, avocados, spinach, peas, asparagus, mushrooms, and spirulina are a great addition to any B-vitamin-deficient diet. The following ACV tonic can also help you ensure your vitamin B levels stay safe and stable. Spirulina is an algae supplemental powder that is readily available in most health food stores and many local grocery stores.

TO MAKE A DRINK, COMBINE:

1 tablespoon ACV

1 cup water

1 teaspoon spirulina

1 pear, cored

Combine all ingredients in a blender (with ice if desired) and blend until desired consistency is achieved. Drink daily.

Each B vitamin plays a different role in helping your body:

- B_1 **(thiamine)**—Involved in the synthesis of energy from carbohydrates and RNA and DNA production. Deficiency leads to neurological complications, pain, and sensory issues.
- B_2 **(riboflavin)**—Aids in energy production for electrolyte transport, and is involved in the transformation of fatty-acid molecules into energy. Deficiency leads to ariboflavinosis, in which cracked lips, sensitivity to sunlight, and a sore throat lead to more serious health conditions.
- B_3 **(niacin)**—Involved in the energy-transfer reactions in

the metabolism of glucose, fat, and alcohol. Deficiency can result in aggression, insomnia, weakness, and dermatitis.

- **B$_5$ (pantothenic acid)**—Involved in the oxidation of fatty acids and carbs, as well as the synthesis of amino acids, fatty acids, ketones, cholesterol, and steroid hormones. The most common sign of deficiency is acne.
- **B$_6$ (pyridoxine)**—Involved in the metabolism of amino acids and lipids, and the synthesis of neurotransmitters and hemoglobin. Deficiency results in microcytic anemia, depression, dermatitis, hypertension, and water retention.
- **B$_7$ (biotin)**—Involved in the metabolism of lipids, proteins, and carbohydrates and metabolizing energy, amino acids, and cholesterol. Deficiency results in impaired growth and neurological disorders in infants.
- **B$_9$ (folic acid)**—Ensures normal cell division, especially during pregnancy, and plays a major role in the production of red blood cells. Deficiency results in elevated levels of homocysteine, and can result in birth defects.
- **B$_{12}$ (various cobalamins)**—Involved in the cell metabolism of carbohydrates, proteins, and lipids, and the production of red blood cells in bone marrow, nerve sheaths, and proteins. Deficiency results in memory loss and cognitive defects.

21 Avoid Vitamin A Deficiencies

Vitamin A acts as a powerful antioxidant that can help improve your immunity and boost your body's ability to replenish healthy cells. (Antioxidants fight off dangerous cancerous cell changes and are found in the foods we consume.) Vitamin A is actually consumed in the form of beta carotene and then converted to vitamin A in the body. People who eat a diet lacking adequate nutritional foods such as deep green vegetables, fibrous fruits, and fruits and vegetables of bright hues (the bright oranges, reds, and greens indicate high values of beta carotene) may find themselves deficient in vitamin A. Supplements for the valuable vitamin are available, but they do not contain beta carotene. Thus, consuming a diet rich in the beta-carotene-packed foods offers up a double dose of health by including beta carotene *and* vitamin A benefits. Skipping supplements and opting for more natural sources of vitamin A—such as ACV—is becoming more and more common among vitamin A–deficient consumers.

Try this drink:

TO MAKE A DRINK, COMBINE:

- 1 tablespoon ACV
- 1 cup almond milk, vanilla flavored
- ½ baked sweet potato, skin removed
- 1 teaspoon cinnamon
- ½ teaspoon ground cloves

Combine all ingredients in a blender and blend until desired consistency is achieved. Drink daily to experience the health-boosting benefits of vitamin A.

22 Boost Essential Amino Acids

Amino acids are commonly referred to as the building blocks of proteins, but these powerhouses don't stop their work there! They also:

- Act as essential players in all metabolic processes
- Have control of or involvement in all of the body's cells, from the communication between the brain and the body to the efficiency of the digestive system

Of the twenty amino acids, there are ten we synthesize or make on our own; these self-made amino acids are referred to as *nonessential amino acids* because it is not essential for us to include them in our diet. The other ten amino acids are those that we cannot produce on our own and are referred to as *essential amino acids*; it is this group of amino acids that must be consumed through a diet of plant-based foods, such as soy beans. Plants are the only biological group able to create these amino acids due to their unique biochemical structure, which is unlike that of animals. Because the body doesn't store amino acids in the same way that it stores fat or carbohydrates, we have to consume them daily. If we fail to consume adequate amounts of even one type of essential amino acid, the body starts to experience a degradation in proteins, which means all of the systems in which the depleted amino acid acts suffer.

By integrating apple cider vinegar into your daily diet, your body experiences a boost in amino acid functioning in two ways.

1. Apple cider vinegar's beneficial addition of multiple vitamins, minerals, enzymes, and phytochemicals helps the body to better absorb and process the essential amino acids within the foods you eat.

2. The additional amino acids found in organic, unfiltered ACV add to the dietary amino acids you ingest through your daily diet, ensuring your amino acid intake is adequate to prevent deficiency.

TO MAKE AN AMINO ACID–BOOSTING DRINK, COMBINE:

1   cup water

1–2   teaspoons ACV

Consume the mixture three times daily (ideally, morning, noon, and evening) to ensure your body is optimizing its amino acid intake and processing.

23 Ease Symptoms of Irritable Bowel Syndrome (IBS)

Irritable bowel syndrome (IBS) is characterized by uncomfortable digestion due to pain experienced with the intestinal muscle spasms needed for moving food through the colon. In addition to the pain experienced from the process of digestion, those who endure IBS also experience diarrhea, constipation, or both, on a regular basis. IBS has no known cause, and the treatments for the condition range from natural to pharmaceutical and number in the hundreds. As with many of the pharmaceutical answers to medical conditions, the medicines created to treat IBS have certain undesirable side effects that have prompted IBS sufferers to seek more natural alternatives.

With specific acids that neutralize digestive enzymes and stomach acid, pectin for fiber that softens and bulks stools for easier passage through the colon, and antiviral and antibacterial properties that help to maintain an optimal balance of bacteria in the gut, apple cider vinegar is growing in popularity as a natural IBS pain reliever. Packed with beneficial vitamins, minerals, enzymes, and natural phytochemicals that act to protect your immunity on a cellular level, ACV is not only an inexpensive and easily attainable remedy; it's simple to integrate into any lifestyle.

TO MAKE A PREVENTIVE TONIC, COMBINE:

1   tablespoon ACV

2   cups water

Sip the concoction prior to meals to help prevent IBS.

TO MAKE A TONIC TO HELP CURRENT SYMPTOMS, COMBINE:

2–4   teaspoons ACV

1   cup water

Sip over the course of a 30-minute period.

24 Add Fiber to Your Diet

"Roughage" is just another term for fiber, and most people would benefit greatly from having more of it in their daily diet. The number of benefits provided by fibrous foods is plentiful:

- Reduction of hunger and reduced calorie consumption
- Better controlled blood glucose levels
- Lower incidences of heart disease

By simply adding more roughage to your daily diet, you can enjoy a number of these benefits.

There are two types of dietary fiber:

1. **Insoluble fiber**—Found in fruits, vegetables, nuts, and grains, and is indigestible. While it does move through the digestive process, it is not absorbed and simply passes through. Because the body is unable to digest this fiber, it leads to a longer duration of feeling full after a meal or snack and leads to a more even blood sugar level (when you eat non-fiber-rich foods, your blood sugar level can spike and dip). Even though it leads to a slower digestive time, this fiber is thought to reduce the incidence of constipation, hemorrhoids, heart disease, and colorectal cancers.

2. **Soluble fiber**—Found in fruits, nuts, oats, and barley, this type of fiber interacts with water by forming a gel-like substance. This gel-like fiber turns ½ cup of dry oatmeal into 1½ cups when mixed with water. The gel produced by soluble fiber lubricates stools and helps to flush the colon of unhealthy bacteria and waste as it passes through, by collecting bits of undigested debris.

While fiber products are readily available, apple cider vinegar is an all-natural alternative.

TO MAKE A DRINK THAT HELPS ADD FIBER TO YOUR DIET, COMBINE IN A BLENDER:

2   cups water

1–2   teaspoons ACV

1   Fuji apple, cored

Blend until apple is emulsified and all ingredients are well combined.

Drink daily.

25 Enhance a Vegetarian Diet

The most common risk associated with a vegetarian diet is the possibility of missing out on certain essential nutrients needed to optimize the body's functioning. There are a couple of specific vegetarian groups that are categorized by what is avoided in their diets:

- A "vegetarian" (who eats no meat, but includes dairy products, eggs, and animal products)
- A "vegan" (who avoids all products derived from animals)

Vegetarian and vegan diets that exclude meat and animal products *are* certainly able to provide the essential micronutrients our bodies need. By planning vegetarian or vegan meals that provide all of the necessary vitamins and minerals, you can meet all dietary needs. Adding apple cider vinegar to a vegetarian or vegan diet provides the following benefits:

- It aids in the absorption of macronutrients (carbohydrates, proteins, and fats) and micronutrients consumed in the daily diet. With this optimized absorption, amino acid absorption and processing is also optimized, ensuring proper cell functioning and growth.
- The fiber naturally occurring in ACV aids in digestion, reducing difficult digestion issues commonly associated with the plant-based foods included in the vegetarian diet.
- Naturally occurring phytonutrients and enzymes containing antiviral and antibacterial properties are also included in ACV, boosting the immune system of a vegetarian diet (which can be lacking in immunity-boosting vitamins normally found in dairy products and healthy meats).

TO MAKE A CALCIUM-BOOSTING DRINK, COMBINE IN A BLENDER:

½ tablespoon ACV

1 cup coconut or almond milk

Your favorite fruits and spices

Drink daily.

Chapter 2: **TOTAL WELLNESS**

When you utilize nature's medicine cabinet by optimizing your diet and focusing your daily consumption of foods on natural, whole varieties, you maximize your overall health and wellness by naturally supplying ample amounts of essential vitamins, minerals, and protective elements. This is a well-known fact. When you suffer from medical conditions and health-depleting illnesses, it can be easy to fall victim to the marketing ploys that drug manufacturers spend billions of dollars to design to ensure that you choose their products for calming symptoms or curing ailments.

But, if you prefer to seek out natural treatments over the pharmaceutically produced pills and potions that promise to cure illnesses and calm symptoms, you are one of the millions of consumers who have decided to turn to nature for better health! Not only can apple cider vinegar provide you with relief from everyday life-altering symptoms; it can improve your overall health and return you to the quality of life you dream of.

Many health conditions result from damage to the body's cells, deficiencies of nutrients needed for optimal system functioning, or extensive multisystem dysfunction that results in a domino-effect-like series of illnesses. Whether you suffer from diabetes and poor circulation, chronic inflammation and muscle stiffness, or even depression and anxiety, you can easily find yourself on a seemingly downward spiral of ill health. The good news is that when you get your systems back on track, focus your lifestyle and diet on healthy activities and whole foods, and implement a simple ACV regimen in your daily routine, you can take control of your health and get back to living . . . naturally!

Vitamin deficiencies can wreak havoc on your body by affecting the functioning of one system that affects another and another and so on, leading to a breakdown in multiple areas of the body. If you consider the body as parts of a whole, you can see why it's necessary to not simply treat just one symptom or one illness but rather treat the body as an integrative series of systems functioning to assist and support each other. By ensuring your body is receiving quality nutrients that provide all of the body's systems with ample supplies of what they need, you can remedy not one but many health issues at the same time.

26 Detoxify—The Natural Way

Apple cider vinegar has long been used as an effective detoxification tool, and for good reason! The main goals of a detox are to:

1. Cleanse the system of toxins, such as air and environmental pollutants, processed ingredients from foods, and chemicals from everyday products

2. Assist the body's organ systems in ridding the body of built-up waste

3. Replenish the body's stores of valuable vitamins and minerals essential for optimal functioning

An apple cider vinegar detox offers all of these benefits, and more, making it the perfect addition to a detoxification plan. It's simple, easy, and effective, and sure to leave you feeling rejuvenated, refreshed, and healthfully replenished! A natural, organic option that offers a variety of vitamins, minerals, and essential nutrients, ACV can be the perfect supplement that offers cleansing properties and restorative vitamins and minerals, everything you need to ensure you're providing your body with what it needs during a detoxification program.

TO MAKE A SUPPLEMENTAL DETOX DRINK, COMBINE:

1 tablespoon ACV

2 cups water

Drink the ACV mixture in the morning, afternoon, and evening. If your detox includes meals, drink the mixture 30 minutes prior to meals.

A typical detoxification plan lasts for one to seven days, and sometimes includes whole foods. Usually, you start by consuming only liquids, then you might slowly introduce whole foods. While most people opt to use a liquid-only cleanse in order to allow the body to rid itself of waste and start "fresh" after the detox is completed, there is a big benefit to including certain whole foods: Adding fiber will assist the body's digestive system in purging waste.

A detox plan that includes ACV provides so many advantages:

- Beneficial enzymes and acetic acid that help neutralize stomach acids
- Added fiber, which forms a gel in the gut and helps to remove toxins and waste
- Helps the liver and other organs that play essential roles in detoxifying the body effectively remove toxins while replenishing stores of vitamins and minerals needed to operate more effectively
- Powerful antioxidants that boost the immune system and safeguard one's health throughout the detoxification process
- Many people who consume ACV have reported a boost in energy levels, which becomes important during any fast

27 Improve a Diabetic Lifestyle

Diabetics focus much of their attention on consuming foods that provide quality nutrition and assist in maintaining stable blood sugar levels. While many diabetics find this dietary focus a little overwhelming when starting out, the process of selecting specific foods that are diabetes-friendly becomes second nature soon enough. Regardless of whether one has been diagnosed as prediabetic or is a confirmed type 1 or type 2 diabetic, many patients suffering from diabetic symptoms can find relief by simply adding apple cider vinegar to their daily diet regimen.

Packed with enzymes and acetic acid that aid in maintaining the body's blood glucose levels at optimal numbers for longer durations, apple cider vinegar has shown to improve the diabetic lifestyle in the following ways:

- Reducing the frequency of blood sugar spikes and dips.
- Providing a feeling of fullness lasting long after the completion of a meal; diabetics also report consuming a more regular diet of smaller, more frequent meals, resulting in a more stable blood sugar level.
- Helping diabetics experience less frequent bouts of diarrhea and constipation that can result from the diabetic diet or medications prescribed to control the condition. The fast-acting acetic acid and pectin in ACV helps the body's digestive system maintain normal functioning by adding bulk to stools and lubricating the digestive system to move waste more effectively.

Because ACV can affect potassium and magnesium levels, it's important to talk to your doctor about whether ACV might be right for you. If so, try this tonic:

TO MAKE A DRINK, COMBINE:

2   teaspoons ACV

¼   cup organic, unfiltered apple juice

1   cup water

Consume the mixture upon rising in the morning, prior to lunch, and prior to bedtime.

28 Help Safeguard Against Cancer

Cancer is one of the most dreadful diseases of modern times. Cancers of all types affect people of every gender, age, and ethnicity. While there are known factors that contribute to the development of cancer cells—such as genetics, sun exposure, smoking, and other environmental and lifestyle factors—sometimes, there's no advance warning. Cancer treatments come with many very difficult side effects that range from hair loss to extreme nausea and fatigue. Because of the increasing awareness of cancer and its treatments, many people are looking for natural preventive measures that can be taken in an attempt to safeguard their health from cancerous developments. One such natural method is vitamin C.

Though it may seem like a simple vitamin couldn't possibly affect a disease as serious as cancer, it can. Vitamin C can influence cancer in the following ways:

- Acts as a powerful antioxidant that can stop cancerous changes within cells by reversing the damage done by free radicals that cause the cancerous changes.
- Vitamin C infusions have shown to drastically improve the overall health of some cancer patients, improving the effectiveness of cancer treatments and helping some patients reach the point of remission.
- Improves the effectiveness of the immune system and aids in the body's ability to absorb the essential vitamins and minerals required to function properly.

FOR A DRINK THAT WILL HELP BOOST VITAMIN C LEVELS, COMBINE THESE INGREDIENTS IN A BLENDER UNTIL DESIRED CONSISTENCY IS REACHED:

1   cup freshly squeezed orange juice

½   cup freshly squeezed grapefruit juice

1   tablespoon ACV

1   frozen banana

Drink daily.

29 Stop the Hiccups

There are, seemingly, millions of theories about how or why we get hiccups, and just as many theories of how to cure them. Medically, the most accepted theory as to what happens during a bout of the hiccups is a repetitive spasm of the diaphragm. The diaphragm is a dome-shaped muscle separating the chest from the abdomen, and the spasm that occurs in the diaphragm leads to an immediate reactive closure of the vocal chords, creating the "hiccup" sound. While the hiccups are a harmless condition, they can be very annoying, and in some cases very uncomfortable. While, for most, a bout of the hiccups generally lasts for only a few minutes, there have been reported cases of hiccups lasting for days, weeks, and even months! Whether the cause is nerves, eating or drinking too fast, or the body's natural attempt to deliver more oxygen to the brain, the hiccups are one more condition that apple cider vinegar can help!

Because of its strong taste, pungent aroma, and powerful effects within the digestive system, apple cider vinegar causes immediate physical reactions that many people credit in its effectiveness as a cure for hiccups. While the medical support for ACV as a cure for hiccups may not be available just yet, decades and generations of avid ACV users are happy to attest to the effectiveness as a hiccup cure. What do you have to lose?

TO MAKE A DRINK, COMBINE:

1   tablespoon ACV

1   tablespoon water

Consume between hiccups.

30 Clear Up a Stuffy Nose

Whether the cause is allergies, a common cold, or a vicious virus, a stuffy nose is an awful symptom to experience. Cleverly created marketing strategies are designed to bombard stuffy-nose-sufferers with the temptation of relief in a bottle. Desperate consumers opt for these quick fixes at the height of cold and flu or allergy seasons, unknowingly getting more than they bargained for. Pills, drinks, and sprays that act to unstuff a stuffy nose are created using combinations of steroids, stimulants, and chemicals that aid in drying up the nose. While these over-the-counter treatments can be effective, the majority of them contain powerful ingredients that produce harmful side effects that can wreak havoc on your body and mind. From jitters and endless energy to symptoms that return right away, over-the-counter remedies can be more hazardous than helpful. This is just one of the reasons consumers are turning to natural remedies instead of pharmaceutically created options.

Apple cider vinegar is one of the tried-and-true natural alternatives that have been used to clear up stuffy noses for centuries. All it takes is a sniff of apple cider vinegar to experience the effectiveness of the tonic's ability to clear the sinuses! The enzymes and antiviral properties contained in ACV can be effective in relieving a stuffy nose in three ways:

TO MAKE A DRINK, COMBINE:

1   tablespoon ACV

1   cup hot water

Drink as often as needed to resolve symptoms.

TO MAKE A STEAM TREATMENT, BOIL:

4   cups water

1   cup ACV

Simply drape a towel over your head as you lean over the pot to trap the steam. Inhale the vapors.

TO USE AN ACV TONIC AS A NETI POT FLUID, COMBINE:

1   cup water

2   teaspoons ACV

To use, drain down the sinuses and through the throat.

31 Ease a Sore Throat

A sore throat can come on unexpectedly, and can be an isolated experience or a symptom of a far more serious condition. Pharyngitis, which means "inflammation of the throat," is the medical term for a sore throat. While it has a number of causes that range from infection to irritation, a sore throat should be treated as soon as the scratchiness, irritation, and pain arise. Whether the crux of the issue is viral or bacterial, apple cider vinegar is a natural remedy that provides nutritional benefits that calm from the inside out. Containing a number of naturally occurring vitamins, minerals, enzymes, and antioxidants—along with antiviral and antibiotic properties—that work together in soothing a sore throat, ACV in its natural, unfiltered, organic state can perform the job of a number of medications all on its own!

TO MAKE A DRINK, COMBINE:

- 1 cup warmed water
- 1 tablespoon ACV
- 1 teaspoon honey (if creating a tonic to drink)

Gargle the mixture by ¼-cup gulps, or drink the tonic warmed with the added teaspoon of honey to kill germs in the mouth and throat as you swallow the mixture.

The vitamin C contained in ACV also provides immunity-boosting effects by fending off illness while also strengthening the immune system.

32 Soothe Sinusitis

Sinusitis, also known as a sinus infection, is a condition caused by a microorganism (in the form of a bacteria, virus, or fungus) that grows within the air pockets of the sinus and causes a blockage. While some experience sinusitis once in a while, many sufferers find they have chronic sinus problems. As a result of the infection, the sinuses swell and begin producing an abnormal amount of mucus. As the infection persists, the inflammation and mucus cause the traditional sinusitis symptoms of headaches, facial tenderness, sinus pressure and pain, fever, dark and cloudy nasal discharge, stuffiness, sore throat, cough, and even toothaches. While many cases of sinusitis require antibiotics, some sinusitis sufferers can find relief long before the infection has grown to the point of requiring prescription medications. Over-the-counter relievers are effective in soothing sore throats, relieving pain and fevers, and drying up mucus, but they can also deliver undesirable side effects. For sinusitis sufferers choosing to use natural remedies before turning to more extreme measures, apple cider vinegar is the perfect option.

Containing antibacterial and antiviral properties, apple cider vinegar is packed with essential antioxidants, vitamins, and minerals that combine to combat infections and soothe symptoms. Reinforcing the body's immune system with loads of natural vitamin C, ACV provides support to a sinusitis sufferer by alleviating the symptoms, pinpointing the cause of the condition, and repairing the immune system.

TO MAKE A SOOTHING DRINK TO COMBAT THE SOURCE OF SINUSITIS (BACTERIAL, VIRAL, OR OTHERWISE), COMBINE:

1 tablespoon ACV

1 cup hot water

Drink three times daily.

TO MAKE A STEAM TREATMENT, COMBINE IN A POT:

1 cup ACV

4 cups water

Inhale the vapors as the steam is produced.

33 Combat High Cholesterol

Most people are unaware that cholesterol is actually a *good* thing that the body needs in order to function properly. Cholesterol helps the body produce and process vitamin D, digestive bile, and a number of hormones. Cholesterol is ever-present in the blood and only becomes a problem when there is too much of this "good thing." Contributing to the development of serious conditions like heart disease and stroke, uncontrolled cholesterol levels can result in serious health problems and complications. Comprised of a number of factors including the levels of LDL (the "bad" cholesterol), HDL (the "good" cholesterol), and triglycerides in the blood, your cholesterol levels can be checked with a simple blood test that determines if you have healthy or unhealthy levels. A number of factors including age, family history, diet, and lifestyle habits (smoking, alcohol consumption, etc.) can all play a part in affecting cholesterol levels. By taking an active role in minimizing the contributing factors to high cholesterol levels, you can reduce your risk of developing the dangerous condition.

Loaded with magnesium, potassium, vitamins A, B, and C, and a number of enzymes that assist in maintaining overall health, apple cider vinegar also provides an important element called pectin that helps the body rid itself of excess cholesterol. Pectin binds to excess cholesterol in the digestive system and transports it out of the body as waste. By removing excess cholesterol, the body experiences a healthier level of cholesterols and can better maintain those levels.

TO MAKE A CHOLESTEROL-COMBATING TONIC, COMBINE:

1 teaspoon ACV

1 cup water

Drink twice daily.

As with most health issues, there are a number of prescription medications available for the treatment of high blood pressure. As with most medications, though, they often come with undesirable side effects that can seriously impact your day-to-day life. Because of the serious side effects of these drugs, many people are choosing to try to treat their high blood pressure more naturally. Talk to your doctor about what approach is right for you.

34 Reduce Bad Breath

Everyone gets bad breath now and then. It can be due to a number of factors, such as diet, hygiene, and lifestyle habits such as smoking. While some cases of bad breath are the result of serious illnesses and health conditions, the average case of bad breath is due to germs in the mouth and throat. Brushing your teeth regularly and using a mouthwash may seem like a perfect solution for bad breath, but when it comes to killing germs, products on the market are sometimes ineffective, and most contain harsh chemicals that are questionable for consumption. Check the label on yours—you might see warnings like "do not swallow" or "not safe for consumption"! That warning probably makes you reconsider the over-the-counter bad breath remedies and opt for a more natural solution.

Apple cider vinegar provides antiviral, antibacterial, and antiseptic properties, meaning that is effective in killing viruses, bacteria, and germs. Apple cider vinegar's ability to kill the bacteria and germs within the mouth, on the teeth, and in the gums makes it the perfect solution. **An important note:** Because of the strength of the acids in ACV, it is unsafe to consume undiluted (in order to protect the teeth from being stripped of their protective enamel). Diluted, though, this natural home remedy can be used as a mouth rinse and a gargle to effectively kill off the bad-breath-causing germs and bacteria.

TO MAKE A MOUTH RINSE, COMBINE:

2   teaspoons ACV

½ cup water

Swish in the mouth for 15–20 seconds before spitting.

TO MAKE A GARGLE, COMBINE:

2   teaspoons ACV

½ cup water

Gargle the mixture for 20–30 seconds at a time, repeating as often as necessary.

35 Fend Off Exhaustion

You've no doubt experienced "normal" exhaustion—for example, when you've undergone strenuous activity for long durations, had extensive exposure to the heat, or endured excessive hours without sleep. "Abnormal" exhaustion is considered to be feelings of fatigue when the sufferer has engaged in no such strenuous activity or has not been exposed to environmental factors that would contribute to exhaustive feelings. Whether the exhaustive experience is acute or chronic, many sufferers turn to everyday remedies such as caffeinated beverages like coffee or tea, or more extreme over-the-counter stimulants. Coffees and teas are sometimes effective in suddenly stimulating the senses and are deemed safe and even sometimes beneficial to one's overall health, but they provide only a temporary solution followed by a crash that leads back to the original state of exhaustion. For those experiencing exhaustion on a regular basis, apple cider vinegar offers benefits that target a number of areas serving to remedy the issue—safely and naturally with its plentiful naturally occurring nutrients and enzymes that improve energy levels, mental stability, cognitive functioning,

nerve functioning, and metabolic functioning! How?

- Loaded with natural vitamins like B_{12} and C, apple cider vinegar can boost the body's energy naturally by stimulating the brain, muscles, and tissues without causing jittery or restless symptoms. ACV has been shown to improve the very systems that directly affect energy levels (nervous system for cognition and mental clarity, immune system for overall health maintenance, and metabolism for energy and stamina, to name a few).
- The antioxidants within ACV assist in the repair of the body's cells, aiding in feelings of refreshment and rejuvenation.
- ACV's variety of beneficial vitamins and minerals replenish depleted stores of these essentials and boost immune system functioning.

TO MAKE AN ENERGY-BOOSTING TONIC, COMBINE:

1 tablespoon ACV

2 cups water

¼ cup freshly squeezed orange juice

Consume the mixture three times daily.

36 Relieve Leg Cramps

Cramps in the muscles throughout the body can be caused by issues such as:

- Nutrient deficiencies
- Dehydration
- Excessive wear and tear resulting from exercise or bouts of physical endurance
- Poor circulation

Whether the leg cramps you experience result from one of these possible causes or seem to have been brought on by another factor, your local pharmacy probably boasts a vast array of anti-inflammatory pills, tonics, and topical creams that promise to provide relief. While many of these solutions may be effective, they may provide only a temporary relief and often come with a host of possible undesirable side effects. If you find yourself suffering from leg cramps, try these ACV options.

TO MAKE A QUICK-ACTING TONIC, COMBINE:

1 tablespoon ACV

2 cups water

Drink 1–3 times daily until symptoms subside.

TO MAKE A SOOTHING BATH SOLVENT, COMBINE:

Tub full of warm water

1 cup ACV

Soak in the mixture for up to 30 minutes to relieve lactic acid buildup, stimulate circulation, and remove toxins.

The organic, unfiltered variety can replenish the body's stores of valuable vitamins and minerals that are normally depleted when cramping and muscle soreness occur.

TO MAKE A TOPICAL SOLUTION, DAMPEN A WET TOWEL WITH ACV.

Apply the towel directly to the cramping area of the leg to relieve lactic acid buildup, stimulate circulation, and remove toxins.

Apple cider vinegar contains a number of reparative vitamins and minerals that have been shown to provide pain relief in muscles and joints. Said to improve circulation of the blood, ACV has long been used to alleviate muscle cramping and soreness by stimulating blood flow throughout the body and delivering higher volumes of oxygenated blood to the areas in need.

37 Regulate Blood Sugar

If you tend to binge on carbs, then feel overfull and experience sluggishness, you might be having trouble regulating your blood sugar. High-carb foods cause spikes in the body's blood sugar levels that are then followed by a crash. When it comes to blood sugar regulation, the most commonly prescribed dietary solution is fiber. Acting to maintain steady blood sugar levels and prevent spikes from carbohydrate-rich foods, fiber serves as a natural option in regulating one's blood sugar levels. Apple cider vinegar's natural vitamins, minerals, and enzymes support the body's processes by supplying healthy amounts of immunity-building, blood-cleansing, detoxifying nutrients, along with healthy doses of fiber in the form of pectin. Forming a gel-like substance in the digestive system, pectin provides a sustained feeling of fullness that extends the period of time between meals by reducing hunger—and helping you avoid a carb binge. As an added benefit, ACV also provides enzymes that aid in digestion and help to maintain a steady release of insulin, further supporting the maintenance of steady blood sugar levels.

TO HELP YOU REGULATE BLOOD SUGAR, COMBINE:

1 cup water

1 tablespoon ACV

Drink three times a day.

38 Minimize Yeast Infections

From itching and burning to immediate and urgent needs to urinate to foul-smelling discharge, this unpleasant, yeast-related fungal infection is one that can develop quickly and requires swift treatment, sometimes even requiring antibiotics to clear the infection. Yeast infections can also affect the skin, the intestines, and the mouth, and are caused by an overgrowth of candida. Because the bacteria levels in the body directly affect the production of flora and fungus, doctors often recommend probiotics intended to boost production of the "good" bacteria that can prevent or even treat yeast infections. By regulating bacteria levels internally, you can reduce the incidence of yeast overgrowth and control yeast infections before they start.

With apple cider vinegar, you can effectively treat a yeast infection from the inside out, and minimize symptoms quickly. Its antifungal, antibacterial, and antiseptic qualities can help resolve the internal disruption of yeast overgrowth.

TO MAKE A DRINK, COMBINE:

1   cup water

¼   cup organic pure cranberry juice, not from concentrate

1   tablespoon ACV

Drink every hour until symptoms subside.

TO MAKE A TUB SOAK FOR IMMEDIATE RELIEF, COMBINE:

Tub full of water

2   cups ACV

Soak for up to 30 minutes.

39 Overcome Laryngitis

By consuming apple cider vinegar, you can deliver antiviral, antibacterial, antifungal, and antiseptic properties contained within ACV to the larynx. The following concoctions can provide relief to the irritated area, while the germ-fighting properties kill the sources of irritation, leaving the larynx free of irritants and better suited for recovery.

TO MAKE A DRINK, COMBINE:

1 cup warm water

1 tablespoon ACV

1 teaspoon organic honey

Drink every 30–60 minutes until symptoms subside.

TO MAKE A GARGLE, COMBINE:

½ cup warm water

2–4 tablespoons ACV

Gargle the mixture for 20–30 seconds at a time, repeating as often as necessary.

The gargle can prevent further irritation caused by looming germs, toxins, and debris on the teeth, tongue, gums, and throat; gargling with this solution also minimizes further irritation from postnasal drips that can seep down the back of the throat.

Whether you suffer from allergies, have inhaled environmental toxins, or are dealing with a cold or flu, laryngitis can be your body's reaction to irritants in the larynx. Natural treatments for resolving laryngitis and calming the symptoms that result are becoming more and more appealing, as pharmaceutical companies continue to use chemicals and harsh additions in their treatments. By using apple cider vinegar as a treatment, one can find relief of laryngitis naturally, and without the undesirable side effects that can sometimes accompany over-the-counter medications.

40 Relieve Muscle Stiffness

Lactic acid is the normal byproduct produced by muscles following the processing of essential proteins. The buildup of lactic acid in the muscles is what can cause stiffness and pain in areas such as the neck, back, butt, legs, and arms. While stretching is the most effective way to cure muscle stiffness—because it allows the muscles to literally release the lactic acid into the blood to be carried away as waste—many muscle stiffness sufferers opt for over-the-counter treatments. Unfortunately, most relieve the pain only temporarily, and in some cases even aggravate the condition! Luckily, lactic acid buildup in the muscles can be naturally treated by stretching of the stiff areas and using various apple cider vinegar applications. ACV contains acetic acid and vitamins and minerals that aid in the processing of elements such as lactic acid.

TO MAKE A DRINK, COMBINE:

1 cup water

2 teaspoons ACV

TO MAKE A SOOTHING BATH, COMBINE:

Tub full of water

2 cups ACV

Soaking for up to 30 minutes allows the nutrients, acids, and enzymes in ACV to pull toxins from the body, enabling the body to more effectively rid the muscles and blood of lactic acid buildup.

TO MAKE A TOPICAL TREATMENT, COMBINE IN A BOWL:

1 cup water

¼ cup ACV

Warm the mixture, then submerge a towel in the solution, ring out the excess, and place the towel directly on the site of stiffness for 15 minutes at a time.

41 Reduce Congestion

Sinus congestion and chest congestion are the two most commonly reported types of congestion. With congestion of any type, symptoms can range from headaches and coughs to toothaches and difficulty breathing. Unchecked congestion can also lead to more severe illnesses like sinus infections and pneumonia. Before reaching the point of requiring doctor's visits, prescriptions, or trips to the hospital for chest x-rays and treatment, you can opt for natural cures like ACV, which attacks the source of the problem as well as the symptoms that result. With antibacterial, antifungal, antiviral, and antiseptic properties that kill the source of congestion, ACV can stop an infection and start the road to recovering from congestion almost immediately.

In three simple ways, you can find relief from congestion using apple cider vinegar: ingesting an ACV solution, inhaling the steam from an ACV solution, and bathing in an ACV solution.

TO MAKE A DRINK, COMBINE:

1   cup water

1–2   tablespoons ACV

Drink daily.

Effectively supporting your body's natural healing processes with vitamins, minerals, and phytonutrients, drinking ACV is one of the most effective ways to cure and prevent congestion.

TO MAKE A STEAM TREATMENT, BOIL IN A POT:

4   cups water

1   cup ACV

Inhale the vapors.

This steam treatment helps you open the sinuses and chest, alleviating congestion and calming the irritated areas.

TO MAKE A SOOTHING BATH, COMBINE:

Bath full of water

2–4   cups ACV

Soak for up to 30 minutes.

This bath helps to alleviate congestion by drawing toxins out of the body while also producing moisture-packed vapors for you to inhale.

42 Minimize Allergies

Most commonly caused by irritants in the air, allergic reactions can also be due to exposure to certain stimulants to which the body has adverse effects—anything from pollen to pet dander. A runny nose, itchy eyes, burning or scratchy throat, cough, congestion, and mucus production can all be results of allergic reactions. Because allergy symptoms can be mild enough to be simply bothersome, many people turn to over-the-counter remedies that provide symptomatic relief. Because treating the symptoms alleviates the discomfort without treating the cause of the reaction, many allergy sufferers experience a return of the symptoms once the medication has worn off. In addition to providing only temporary relief as well as rebound effects, many over-the-counter medications have been shown to cause undesirable side effects like fatigue or jitters, or actually exacerbate symptoms by increasing mucus production. Apple cider vinegar can actually help treat *and* prevent allergy symptoms.

By combining the antibacterial, antiviral, and antiseptic properties of apple cider vinegar with natural ingredients like honey and cinnamon that have shown to reduce the instances of histamine-related symptoms, many allergy sufferers have seen drastic improvements in their immune system functioning, the incidences of allergic reactions, and the severity of those reactions.

TO MAKE A SOOTHING DRINK, COMBINE:

1 tablespoon ACV

1 cup warm water

1 teaspoon honey

½ teaspoon cinnamon

Drink up to three times daily while experiencing symptoms, and once daily in the morning for preventive purposes.

Due to an increase in mucus production and an already compromised immune system, many allergy sufferers find themselves progressing from simple allergy symptoms (such as sneezing, runny nose, clear sinus drainage) to developing serious illnesses such as sinus infections (signified by sinus headaches and pressure with stuffy, cloudy sinus mucus) overnight or within a twelve-hour span of time. The preventive drink can help you avoid that situation!

43 Defend Against Cataracts

Quality eyesight is vital to nearly every aspect of everyday life. Taking the steps necessary to safeguard your eye health now will ensure you can continue enjoying activities like reading, sports, and driving for years to come. One of the most commonly experienced eye-related issues is cataracts, and this condition can be helped or hindered by the lifestyle choices you make every day.

Light that enters your eye passes through a lens directly behind your iris, and when the oxidative stress of free radicals damages the cells in this lens, the natural proteins of the lens clump together and make the lens cloudy, hardened, and discolored. This is what we refer to as a cataract. Because free radicals are to blame in causing the cell damage that leads to cataracts, the most effective way to prevent and reverse damage to the eye's lens is to include as many antioxidant-rich foods in the diet as possible. A diet of fruits and vegetables rich in antioxidants—along with ACV—can help your eyes stay healthy. Apple cider vinegar:

- Provides the antioxidants needed to combat oxidative stress that directly affects eye health
- Contains beta carotene, one of the most essential nutrients for eye health, and supports the regeneration of cells in the eyes while safeguarding those same cells from further damage

TO MAKE AN EYE-HEALTH-FRIENDLY DRINK, COMBINE:

1   cup fresh carrot juice
    juice of ¼" ginger
1   tablespoon ACV
Drink daily.

44 Lessen Joint Pain

Pain experienced in the joints can be due to a buildup of toxins within the joint cavity or surrounding muscle and connective tissues. Because it is the toxicity in joints that can result in uncomfortable irritation and inflammation, many over-the-counter medications can be helpful in alleviating symptoms, but may do so only temporarily, treating the symptoms but not the source of the issue. Plus, they can contain harmful chemicals and additives. By treating the cause of the joint pain with ACV instead, you can alleviate the symptoms and prevent the symptoms' return effectively and naturally.

As a pain-relieving alternative to over-the-counter medications, apple cider vinegar provides healing properties that promote the optimal functioning of a number of systems, boosting the body's overall immunity while also focusing on reducing the toxicity of the joints where pain is being experienced. The naturally occurring enzymes and antioxidants within apple cider vinegar act to combat the buildup of the body's waste products that can accumulate in joints and surrounding tissues. These enzymes and antioxidants bind with the toxic substances and flush them out in the blood stream and digestive systems. You can find the aloe vera juice used in this tonic at health food stores and some grocery stores.

TO MAKE A DRINK, COMBINE:

1   cup water
2   tablespoons organic aloe vera juice
1   tablespoon ACV

Drink daily.

TO MAKE AN ON-THE-SPOT TREATMENT, SOAK A WET TOWEL WITH ACV.

Apply to the site of joint pain, allowing the ACV to help draw out toxins from the area. Leave application on the site of joint pain for over an hour. Repeat as needed.

TO MAKE A SOOTHING SOAK, COMBINE:

Tub full of warm water
4   cups ACV

Soak for 30–60 minutes to allow the properties of ACV to draw toxins out of the body naturally, minimizing the pain in the affected areas.

45 Alleviate Foot Fungus

Not only is foot fungus an embarrassing condition; it can be very uncomfortable and challenging to cure. While there are tons of antifungal over-the-counter creams and powerful prescriptions designed to deal with the unsightly condition, many are costly, ineffective, or provide as many uncomfortable side effects as they do results. As more natural alternatives to chemical-laden options become increasingly appealing, apple cider vinegar has become a popular recommendation for treating foot fungus. In its raw, unfiltered form, apple cider vinegar has been shown to relieve skin conditions like foot fungus in two ways: internally and on-site, making it effective as a treatment and also as a preventive measure.

TO MAKE A DRINK THAT BOOSTS THE BODY'S IMMUNE SYSTEM, COMBINE:

1 tablespoon ACV

1 cup water

Drink the concoction daily.

This drink has antiseptic properties that create a healthier environment in which fungi have less opportunity for growth.

TO MAKE A TOPICAL TREATMENT, SOAK A SMALL TOWEL WITH ACV.

Apply to the affected area for 30 minutes at a time.

The antifungal properties within ACV combat the growth of the fungus and prevent the condition from spreading.

46 Reduce Asthma Symptoms

The vitamin C in ACV can be harnessed to treat the symptoms of asthma effectively and with no side effects by providing the beneficial vitamins needed for improved immunity and eased respiratory functioning without chemicals or additives. How? ACV boosts the immune system with its vitamin C and antioxidants. With a more effective immune system, asthma sufferers may be able to better fight certain triggers of the condition, such as environmental irritants, common colds, and respiratory infections. The inhaled and applied treatments using ACV have also shown to be effective in reducing the incidence and severity of asthma symptoms.

TO MAKE A DRINK, COMBINE:

1 tablespoon ACV

¼ cup freshly juiced ginger

1 cup water

Drink daily.

TO MAKE A STEAM TREATMENT, BOIL IN A POT:

4 cups water

1 cup ACV

Inhale the steam produced to open airways and promote better breathing.

TO MAKE A SOOTHING TUB SOAK, COMBINE:

Tub full of warm water

3 cups ACV

Soak for up to 30 minutes. This process can remove toxins from the body, while also producing vapors that may be helpful in alleviating asthma symptoms.

47 Minimize Inflammation

Inflammation is the body's reaction to irritants or buildup of toxins within cells and tissues. Because everything from injuries to the weather can seem to irritate or inflame areas of the body, many people turn to quick and easy methods of relief available at their local drugstore. While over-the-counter pills and ointments may provide temporary relief, ACV can reduce inflammation without harsh chemicals or undesirable side effects.

Diet can have a big impact on inflammation—both positive and negative:

- A diet of whole, natural, nutrient-dense foods can curtail inflammation by minimizing the body's exposure to ingested ingredients that can exacerbate the condition.
- On the other hand, foods containing excessive amounts of sugars, sodium, and fat can contribute to excessive inflammation.

Apple cider vinegar contains a variety of essential vitamins and minerals that directly affect the body's ability to control inflammation from the inside out. Potassium, magnesium, sodium, and a host of other essential minerals can help the body's reaction to irritants that can cause inflammation.

TO MAKE AN INFLAMMATION-CALMING DRINK, COMBINE:

1 cup water

1 tablespoon ACV

Drink daily.

TO MAKE A TOPICAL TREATMENT, SOAK A WARM, WET TOWEL WITH ACV.

Apply it to the inflamed area for 30 minutes at a time until inflammation subsides.

The topical treatment allows the properties within ACV to penetrate the skin, delivering essential nutrients and enzymes to the site of irritation, reducing the inflammation at its source.

48 Combat Food Poisoning

Food poisoning can be the result of ingesting contaminated foods that contain bacteria or viruses, and it can result in symptoms such as abdominal cramps, nausea, vomiting, diarrhea, fever, and dehydration. Because it's not always easy to identify the cause of food poisoning, the most effective forms of treatment are to remain hydrated, flush the body of food, and restore valuable vitamins and minerals that were depleted in the body's natural purging of the bacteria or virus. Apple cider vinegar can be a natural remedy for food poisoning by targeting the source of the condition, as well as assisting the body in replenishing and restoring the body's natural balance of vitamins, minerals, and enzymes.

One of the most detrimental side effects of vomiting and diarrhea is dehydration. Mineral imbalances can occur—making you feel even worse because you need those minerals to assist in fluid regulation. Apple cider vinegar provides these benefits during a bout of food poisoning:

- Delivers ample amounts of acetic acid, enzymes, and minerals like potassium and magnesium that improve the body's processing of sodium and essential electrolytes that rehydrate the body's cells.
- Assists in the absorption of vitamins and minerals in the body's cells.
- Regulates pH within the body.
- Settles the stomach by neutralizing stomach acids and aiding in digestion.
- The fiber provided by the pectin in ACV also assists in the body's flushing of the bacteria or virus causing the food poisoning.

FOR A TUMMY-SOOTHING DRINK, COMBINE:

1 cup water

½ tablespoon ACV

Drink every half-hour until symptoms subside.

49 Battle Insomnia

Insomnia can range from quick disruptions in sleep to extended bouts of sleeplessness, and can be induced by a multitude of conditions, such as:

- Illness
- Depression
- Stress
- Medication side effects
- An unhealthy diet

Regardless of what the cause is, the most effective way to treat insomnia is to improve your overall health and relieve or decrease the body's reactions to internal and/or external stimuli that are affecting the body's natural sleeping patterns. Because insomnia is such a widespread problem today, there are a variety of prescription and over-the-counter medications designed to treat the issue. While they may be able to effectively treat the condition temporarily, most sleep aids focus on treating the issue without treating the cause. This neglect to treat the crux of the issue makes the insomnia sufferer turn to sleep aids for the long term, rather than returning the body to its natural sleep rhythms.

Deficiencies in the essential amino acids, vitamins, and minerals that our bodies use to function properly can make insomnia even worse. Even one deficiency can have a cascading effect, leading to malfunctioning in a number of systems resulting in a variety of reactions, one being insomnia. By consuming a diet rich in vitamins, minerals, and nutrients, you can provide your body's systems with what they need to function correctly. When your body is operating at its best, you can better handle a range of emotions, stress, and anxiety, and allow your body to more effectively deal with external or environmental factors that disrupt sleep.

Apple cider vinegar contains a variety of these essential nutrients and has shown to be effective in returning the body to a more naturally balanced sleep rhythm.

TO MAKE A SLEEP-FRIENDLY DRINK, COMBINE:

1 cup organic, stimulant-free tea (not boiling)

1 tablespoon ACV

Drink daily.

50 Improve Immune System Functioning

ACV's ample supply of key vitamins, minerals, and antioxidants provides immune system support in two ways:

1. Puts less stress on the immune system by reducing the incidence and severity of illnesses it endures.

2. Provides powerful nutrients that have shown to boost the immune system's functioning and effectiveness in protecting the body from external or internal changes that result in illness and disease.

TO MAKE A SIMPLE DRINK, COMBINE:

1 cup water

4 teaspoons ACV

Drink daily.

Loaded with enzymes, vitamins, and nutrients, apple cider vinegar has long been used as a daily preventive treatment to reduce illness. While many of the nutrients in ACV have a profound effect on boosting the body's immune system, its vitamin C content is one of the most effective. Acting as a powerful vitamin and antioxidant, vitamin C not only provides the body with protection against illness-causing agents like germs, viruses, and bacteria, but it also aids the body's cells in repairing, protecting, and regenerating from dangerous changes.

51 Regulate Blood Pressure

High blood pressure can be caused by genetics, a poor diet, excessive stress, or enduring high-pressure situations over extensive periods of time. Whatever the cause may be, high blood pressure is an extremely dangerous health condition that must be dealt with as soon as possible in order to avoid dangerous conditions that can result, such as:

- Stroke
- Congestive heart failure
- Aneurysm
- Heart attack

The possible health conditions that can be a direct result of high blood pressure are frightening and even life-threatening—but there are a number of proactive steps you can take that can reduce your blood pressure naturally. One of these steps is integrating an apple cider vinegar drink into your daily routine.

Simple, all-natural, unfiltered, organic apple cider vinegar can:

- Improve the quality of the blood by removing toxins.
- Improve circulation by boosting metabolic functioning.
- Detoxify the organs and fluids, helping to ensure your body stays free of excess toxins and stress that can complicate the blood flow through the heart and surrounding arteries and veins, leading to heightened blood pressure.

TO MAKE A DRINK TO HELP REGULATE BLOOD PRESSURE, COMBINE:

1 cup water

½ tablespoon ACV

Drink daily.

Other lifestyle changes can have a big effect on blood pressure. For example:

- Adhering to a strict diet of clean, whole foods low in sodium, sugar, and unhealthy fats
- Refraining from caffeinated beverages
- Adding healthy forms of daily exercise

52 Alleviate Headaches

Resulting from dehydration, stress, sinus pressure, muscle tension, elements of a poor diet, or more serious conditions, headaches can be a terrible experience that range from merely frustrating to frequent and debilitating. Many over-the-counter medications and heavy-duty prescriptions are recommended for the treatment of headaches, but these can contain a number of unhealthy elements that could produce undesirable side effects.

Apple cider vinegar is one of the most beneficial natural treatments for a headache because of the vast number of vitamins, minerals, acids, and enzymes it contains. Delivering essential nutrients to the body is an important step in headache treatment and prevention because it ensures that the body's systems have adequate fuel to perform optimally. ACV also helps headaches by:

- Eliminating possible physical causes of headaches such as dehydration
- Improving blood quality by removing toxins
- Improving circulation by boosting metabolic functioning
- Easing muscle tension

TO MAKE A HEADACHE-REDUCING DRINK, COMBINE:

1   cup decaffeinated tea

1   tablespoon ACV

Drink every hour until the headache dissipates.

53 Reduce Swelling

While most instances of swelling occur as a result of injuries or trauma, it can also result from a poor diet or displaced pressure. However the swelling started, as long as serious injuries like fractures and tendon or ligament damage is ruled out, you can effectively alleviate swelling safely and in the comfort of your own home with apple cider vinegar treatments!

Apple cider vinegar can be used to treat swelling by:

- Contributing important vitamins, minerals, enzymes, and acids to detoxifying the body
- Replenishing essential stores of nutrients
- Improving circulation and blood flow to the affected area
- Repairing damaged tissues

TO MAKE A DRINK, COMBINE:

1   cup water

2   tablespoons aloe vera juice

1   tablespoon ACV

Drink daily to reduce swelling and prevent further injury caused by inflammation.

TO MAKE A SOAK THAT CAN RELIEVE SWELLING BY DRAWING TOXINS OUT OF THE BODY, IMPROVING CIRCULATION, AND ASSISTING IN NUTRIENT DELIVERY TO THE AFFECTED AREA, COMBINE:

Tub full of warm water

2–4   cups ACV

Soak for 30–45 minutes, allowing the ACV mixture to penetrate the affected area and treat it from the inside out.

TO MAKE A SPOT TREATMENT, SOAK A WASHCLOTH WITH:

1   cup ACV

½   cup water

Sit with the swollen area elevated, and drape the washcloth over the affected area for 30 minutes at a time every hour until the swelling subsides.

54 Whiten Teeth

Countless commercials on television, in magazines, and online constantly remind us that our teeth should be whiter. One quick trip to the drugstore to purchase a teeth-whitening kit can easily turn into an excruciatingly long tour of the vast number of products on the market that promise "visible results" in weeks, days, or even as short as one hour. These can cost anywhere from a few dollars to more than a hundred, not to mention the teeth-whitening services offered by dentists that can cost thousands and take up loads of time. In addition to the hits to your wallet and your schedule, the chemicals contained in these teeth-whitening products can leave you with exceptionally sensitive teeth that are affected by hot and cold foods and drinks, and even breathing through your mouth! Forget about those treatments and instead turn to apple cider vinegar for a teeth whitener that's inexpensive, natural, and quick.

With powerful acids and enzymes that are able to effectively remove stains, kill germs, and promote a proper pH balance in the mouth, apple cider vinegar has long been used to improve the health of the teeth, gums, and tongue, but it can also be used to whiten and brighten teeth. **An important note:** Only use ACV as a whitening agent in its diluted form, safeguarding the enamel on your teeth from being stripped away.

TO MAKE AN ACV TEETH-WHITENING SYSTEM, COMBINE:

¼ cup ACV

¼ cup warm water

First, swish and spit a mouthful of the mixture to prep your teeth for whitening.

Next, soak your toothbrush in the mixture and brush your teeth daily as you would normally, making sure to cover all areas of the teeth.

Finally, brush with your normal toothpaste as you would routinely.

Performing this routine daily will yield visible results in a matter of a few days to a few weeks without adverse side effects.

55 Prevent Bone Loss

Most people know that calcium is vital in maintaining bone quality. You may not know, however, that you also need to make sure that your body can properly absorb the calcium you take in. In fact, a number of recent studies have highlighted the importance of calcium absorption in overall health. Magnesium is a key mineral in the calcium-absorption process. Combining magnesium and calcium in your diet can help you prevent bone loss and make sure your calcium is being absorbed.

Packed with essential nutrients that promote bone health such as calcium, magnesium, and vitamin C, apple cider vinegar is an all-in-one product that provides minerals to prevent osteoporosis, and it also assists in the body's absorption and utilization of those minerals. ACV's vitamin C and powerful antioxidants also help to shield you from illnesses that can interfere with an active lifestyle that is so highly recommended in maintaining bone health.

TO MAKE A BONE-PROTECTING DRINK, COMBINE:

1 cup almond milk

1 tablespoon ACV

Drink daily.

56 Provide Relief from Shingles

Anyone who has ever experienced shingles knows how painful an experience it can be. The condition is caused by the virus varicella-zoster, which lies dormant in the nerve tissues surrounding the brain and spinal cord following a case of the chicken pox. If you've had chicken pox, the virus is in your body and can develop into shingles at any time. In fact, more than 1 million people are affected by shingles every year! Most commonly, sufferers report that the virus shows up mildly at first, with symptoms of mild pain, burning, or itching before turning into an extremely painful or itchy rash of red, bumpy, or lesion-like spots that can cover any portion of the body from head to toe. Even the simplest task, like putting on clothes, becomes painful. Normally, the virus becomes active during a period of high stress or anxiety, and its effect can be anywhere from mild to severe and lasts for one week to several months.

TO MAKE A PREVENTIVE DRINK, COMBINE:

1 cup water

1 tablespoon ACV

Drink daily.

Due to the antiviral properties contained within ACV, many people promote this all-natural method for preventing viral infections of all kinds, as well as shingles.

IF YOU ARE EXPERIENCING SHINGLES NOW, MAKE A DRINK FOR IMMEDIATE RELIEF BY COMBINING IN A BLENDER (ADD ICE IF YOU PREFER):

1 cup green tea

½ cup strawberries, blueberries, or raspberries

1 tablespoon ACV

Blend until all ingredients are well combined and desired consistency is achieved. Drink up to three times daily to fight the viral infection and speed the healing process.

TO MAKE A SOOTHING SOAK THAT CAN PROVIDE RELIEF OF THE BURNING, ITCHING PAIN THAT IS SYMPTOMATIC WITH A SHINGLES OUTBREAK, COMBINE:

Tub full of warm water

2–4 cups ACV

Soaking for 30 minutes, three times daily, has shown to provide relief from the painful symptoms resulting from shingles. In addition, a shingles sufferer can get topical relief with the following:

TO MAKE A SPOT TREATMENT FOR RASH SITES, COMBINE:

½ cup warm water

½ cup ACV

Apply towels soaked with mixture directly to the affected areas for 30 minutes at a time as often as necessary.

These methods have shown to be quite effective in relieving the physical symptoms of shingles, while also minimizing the length of the virus's infection and resulting symptoms.

57 Relieve Earaches

With powerful antibacterial, antiviral, and antiseptic properties, apple cider vinegar can be used as an effective agent in getting rid of ear pain. Delivering powerful nutrients that also contribute to the healing process by killing the infection, reducing inflammation, and minimizing the pain that results, ACV can be an effective preventive measure as well.

TO MAKE EARDROPS, COMBINE:

¼ cup ACV

⅛ cup water

Warm the solution to body temperature. Drop the solution into your ear for 10 minutes at a time, allow to seep out slowly, and repeat every hour as needed. This process can be repeated multiple times per day, as needed, to reduce pain resulting from the infection.

TO MAKE A DRINK THAT CAN BE USED FOR PAIN RELIEF OR AS A PREVENTIVE MEASURE, COMBINE:

1 cup water

1 tablespoon ACV

For pain relief, drink three times daily until the earache subsides. Drink once daily after the infection has cleared as a preventive measure.

An earache is an uncomfortable condition that can be caused by bacterial or viral infections of the ear canal or any of the outerlying areas. By acting swiftly to kill infections that could be causing the earache, you can minimize the painful symptoms that result as well as the duration of the earache. In order to restore health to the ear's affected area, many earache sufferers turn to over-the-counter medications that can contain harmful chemicals and additives. Not only can this cause damage to the ear or further aggravate the condition; it is important to keep in mind that the ear and its canals to the inner workings of the body are delicate, making some wary of using chemically created products for relief.

58 Prevent Gingivitis

Gingivitis is an infection of the gums and interior of the mouth caused by germs and bacteria. While the original condition takes hold in your mouth, the resulting illnesses can be widespread throughout the body. Shockingly, gingivitis can affect your bones, blood, and heart, creating a number of serious conditions that can require anything from antibiotics to extended hospital stays for effective treatments.

While there are a number of effective products available that combat bacteria in your mouth, many are strong enough to kill the "good" bacteria as well, leaving your mouth susceptible to infections, disease, or illnesses that would normally be prevented by the helpful bacteria. A two-step approach to minimizing only harmful bacteria in the mouth while also improving immune system functioning is the most effective prevention and treatment for safeguarding optimal oral health. Apple cider vinegar is the perfect ingredient for this two-step, at-home treatment.

TO MAKE A SAFE AND EFFECTIVE MOUTH RINSE, COMBINE:

¼ cup water

½ cup ACV

Swish in the mouth for 30 seconds prior to brushing, storing the remaining mixture for later use.

ACV's powerful antiseptic, antibacterial, and antiviral properties will attack infectious organisms while leaving helpful bacteria in the mouth unscathed.

Internally, you can boost the body's immune system, bettering its ability to fight infections with an ACV drink.

TO MAKE A DRINK, COMBINE:

1 cup water

1 tablespoon ACV

Consume the tonic daily.

This two-step ACV treatment will ensure your mouth and body remain free of the harmful, health-threatening bacteria and germs that can lead to gingivitis.

59 Ease Backaches

Backaches can affect every aspect of your daily life. Sitting, standing, walking, driving, and performing the simplest of tasks can become painful activities when you're suffering from a backache. Whether the cause is in the muscles, tissues, bones, or nerves, apple cider vinegar can provide you with the relief you need. Rich in minerals and vitamins that can deliver numerous benefits to multiple systems of the body, ACV has long been used to fight inflammation, which is the most common cause of backaches. ACV provides specific relief to backache sufferers by supplying ample amounts of those essential nutrients needed to repair and restore health to the systems most affected during backaches. Forgo the over-the-counter, chemical-laden medications that promise relief, and opt for this natural alternative that not only calms the site of inflammation but also works to optimize the functioning of the systems affected.

Lactic acid buildup in muscles, calcium issues within the bones, and potassium deficiencies in the nervous system are just a few possible causes of backaches that can all be assisted with the nutrients provided by ACV. The calcium, magnesium, and silica in ACV:

- Fight inflammation
- Boost the body's immune system functioning
- Improve blood flow and blood quality
- Assist in pain relief by reducing inflammation

Following are several ways to use ACV to help you deal with backaches.

TO MAKE A DAILY TONIC, COMBINE:

1 cup water

1 tablespoon ACV

Drink daily.

TO MAKE A TOPICAL RELIEF, COMBINE:

Tub full of warm water

2–4 cups ACV

Soak for 30–60 minutes at a time.

Providing relief *and* preventive treatment, ACV has helped countless backache sufferers return to their pain-free daily lives!

60 Help Resolve Kidney and Bladder Issues

The kidneys and bladder play important parts in ridding the body of harmful toxins. Working hard to flush the body's systems of waste products that result from every chemical reaction of the body (of which there are millions every minute, hour, and day!), the kidneys and bladder have a lot of responsibility in safeguarding your health. When these powerhouse organs are compromised in some way, the damaging effects on one's health can be overwhelming, affecting every system's function.

Many simple lifestyle changes can help protect the health of your kidneys and bladder:

- Drink enough water
- Eat a diet rich in nutritious whole foods
- Refrain from harmful lifestyle habits like smoking and drinking excessively
- Exercise daily

These actions will help to boost the functioning of your metabolism, improve blood quality and blood flow, better detoxify the body, and improve immunity, all of which directly affect the kidney and bladder by minimizing the work placed on them.

ACV promotes the proper functioning of these organs by delivering nutrients, acids, and enzymes that:

- Neutralize harmful stomach acids
- Provide fiber for improved digestion
- Maintain a proper balance of helpful bacteria that safeguard the health of the digestive and urinary systems

TO MAKE A DAILY DRINK, COMBINE:

1 cup water

1 tablespoon ACV

Drink daily.

TO CREATE AN ACV SOAK, COMBINE:

Tub of warm water

2   cups ACV

Soak yourself in the solution for
30 minutes once a week.

Delivering protective nutrients
to the urinary system while also
detoxifying the body, these soaks
can help to prevent organisms from
adversely affecting the health of the
kidneys and bladder.

PART 2

BEAUTY

Chapter 3: SKIN

Billions of women around the world help to contribute to the multibillion-dollar industry that focuses on skin care. And, why not? Every day, we're subjected to countless messages that remind us of our wrinkles, blemishes, redness, liver spots, and varicose veins, along with the message that we can be proactive in reversing the aging process and improving our beauty by simply paying a couple dollars here and a few more dollars there on products designed to help us declare victory on the war of skin conditions that make us less appealing. Before spending another penny on the latest and greatest skin-care product, read this amazing section of apple cider vinegar's uses for skin care. Inexpensive, all-natural, organic apple cider vinegar has long been used to repair and restore the health of skin, and this chapter is dedicated to the many applications you can simply and easily implement starting today to effectively renew your skin and feel better about yourself. With no chemicals, additives, or synthetic materials, apple cider vinegar can help you achieve true lasting beauty in the comfort of your own home, replacing the expensive chemical-laden alternatives that can wreak havoc on your skin and do more harm than good.

The best part of apple cider vinegar is what it can supply to your skin in terms of nourishment. Loaded with vitamins that act as potent antioxidants, ACV is able to repair skin damage and provide antioxidant assistance to prevent further damage caused by unhealthy changes within skin cells. Minerals that promote everything from effective blood flow to improved circulation are also important to skin's health and beautiful appearance, making apple cider vinegar even more appealing. Naturally occurring enzymes and acids that combine to keep skin clear and clean without harsh side effects is just one more benefit of this natural ingredient.

61 Tone Your Skin

If you're one of the many people who spends a pretty penny on top-of-the-line skin toners, you may be relieved to hear that you can instead use apple cider vinegar! When it comes to skin treatments, the same elements that make ACV effective in treating overall health conditions make it an excellent product for treating conditions of the skin as well. The purpose of a skin toner is to remove dead skin cells and oil, refreshing the area of the face and revealing a rejuvenated layer of skin that appears clean, clear, and supple. ACV's vitamins and naturally occurring acids are a safe and effective way to improve the look and feel of skin while also restoring the natural balance of oils and pH of the skin.

Specifically, the acetic and malic acids contained within apple cider vinegar improve the health and appearance of the skin by:

- Gently removing dead skin cells
- Balancing the pH levels of the skin
- Removing dirt and oils from the pores
- Treating the causes of acne and unsightly blemishes
- Providing vitamin C–based antioxidant benefits to restore skin cell health and reverse oxidative damage

TO MAKE A SKIN TONER, COMBINE:

½ cup warm water

⅓ cup ACV

Soak a cotton ball in the solution and apply directly to the skin of the face and neck. The remaining mixture can be stored in a dark, cool place in an airtight container.

62 Cleanse Your Pores

Your face is exposed to a number of toxins throughout the day. Airborne elements and tangible dirt and grime adversely affect the appearance and health of your skin. While environmental factors are to blame to an extent, the more common contributor to clogged pores is actually touching your face with your hands—which you likely do dozens of times per day, consciously or subconsciously. When your pores become clogged with unhealthy deposits from your hands, the skin is unable to "breathe" and can develop an oily, greasy, or excessively dry condition.

Many cleansers on the market contain harsh or abrasive components that can aggravate the skin's natural balance of oils and pH, and lead to unhealthy or uncomfortable skin conditions. As a natural alternative to chemical-laden products, apple cider vinegar provides cleansing properties that rid the skin of harmful deposits and keep the skin's pores open and healthy. By restoring the natural pH balance of the skin, ACV has also shown to regulate the oils produced by the skin, resulting in a healthier balance of oil production and minimizing the clogging of pores.

TO MAKE A PORE CLEANSER, COMBINE IN A BOWL:

½ cup warm water

½ cup ACV

Use a facecloth to absorb the liquid, ring out the excess, and gently rub the skin with the towel. Repeatedly rinse and reabsorb the ACV mixture, reapplying the mixture to the skin until the skin looks and feels refreshed and clear.

63 Ease a Sunburn

When the skin is exposed to excessive sunlight, with or without sunblock, the irritation that results is not only uncomfortable and unsightly, but it can be downright dangerous! More and more research directly associates sun exposure to unhealthy or even cancerous growth of the skin cells. If you've got a sunburn, the most effective way to soothe and repair the skin is to apply natural restorative elements that aid in the regeneration and repair of the skin's cells. One of the most effective agents in improving cell health is vitamin C, and many products on the market that claim to improve skin health contain this essential vitamin. While the cosmetic products available temporarily relieve sunburns or improve the look and feel of skin, few contain the combination of elements provided by apple cider vinegar that can improve skin health safely, naturally, and effectively.

Through its healthy acids and enzymes that restore the natural balance of the naturally occurring oils produced by the skin, ACV alleviates the tightening and burning sensations resulting from a sunburn.

Replenishing the vitamin C stores on-site, topical use of ACV also aids in the cell regeneration in the skin while preventing free radical damage that can cause cancerous cell changes.

TO MAKE A SKIN SOAK, COMBINE:

½ cup cool water

½ cup ACV

Apply the ACV mixture directly to the skin on a moist towel or sponge.

TO MAKE A SOOTHING SOAK, COMBINE:

Tub full of water

2 cups ACV

Soak for 30 minutes.

TO MAKE A DRINK, COMBINE:

1 cup water or freshly squeezed orange juice

1 tablespoon aloe vera juice, organic

1 tablespoon ACV

Drink up to three times daily.

By combining these three treatments, you can alleviate the symptoms that result from a sunburn and effectively treat cell damage that resulted from the sun exposure.

64 Minimize Psoriasis

Psoriasis is an uncomfortable and unsightly condition that is thought to be caused by trauma to the skin, stress, smoking, excessive alcohol consumption, sun exposure, and certain medications. Characterized by silvery or red patches of skin that may or may not itch, psoriasis is a noncontagious condition resulting from the body's autoimmune system seeing the skin cells as pathogens and overstimulating the production of skin cells. While many over-the-counter creams can provide relief of psoriasis and/or treat the skin condition, many contain harsh chemicals or produce undesirable side effects that can further irritate the skin. Lifestyle changes that minimize the factors that are assumed to contribute to the condition (such as quitting smoking and minimizing alcohol consumption, sun exposure, and stress) will help improve the effectiveness of any psoriasis treatment.

Apple cider vinegar has become a notable treatment for skin conditions like psoriasis because of the multitude of beneficial elements it can provide internally, as well as to the site of irritation. ACV provides:

- Immunity-boosting vitamin C
- Blood-quality-improving enzymes
- Reparative antioxidant properties

Apple cider vinegar is a natural product that can improve the health of your skin while also maintaining proper functioning of the body's systems that directly support the skin's health.

TO MAKE A TOPICAL TREATMENT, COMBINE:

½ cup water

½ cup ACV

Soak a towel in the solution and apply it directly to the affected area for 30 minutes.

TO MAKE A DRINK THAT SUPPORTS OVERALL SKIN HEALTH, COMBINE:

1 cup water

1 tablespoon ACV

Drink daily.

65 Diminish Eczema

Eczema is a persistent skin irritation characterized by red, rough, patchy areas of skin. Eczema has shown to be aggravated by allergens, leading medical professionals to categorize the condition as an immune disorder. While there is no known cure for eczema, there are many treatments available that have shown to be effective in reducing the frequency of the condition's appearance, as well as minimizing the symptoms that result from the uncomfortable condition. If your eczema is caused by a particular allergen, minimizing your exposure to it should relieve the condition significantly. While there are a number of products on the market designed to calm the symptoms of eczema, apple cider vinegar is a natural remedy worth trying.

Acting as an antibacterial, antifungal, and antiviral agent that also provides essential nutrients and hypoallergenic properties, ACV is able to reduce inflammation on-site, keep the irritated and inflamed area of eczema free of agitating environmental elements, and also help to soothe and repair the skin's cells being affected by the reaction.

TO MAKE A TOPICAL TREATMENT, COMBINE EQUAL PARTS:

water

ACV

Soak a towel in the solution and apply to the affected area for 30 minutes.

TO MAKE A DRINK, COMBINE:

1   cup freshly juiced strawberries

1   tablespoon ACV

Drink daily.

The vitamin C and acetic and malic acids combine to reinforce a healthy immune system and reparation of the skin's cells.

66 Relieve Hemorrhoids

Hemorrhoids are most commonly experienced by the elderly and pregnant women, but they can also strike men and women of all ages. Usually resulting from pushing or straining the bowels while defecating, hemorrhoids are swollen, inflamed veins that can be internal or external, and can be extremely painful or simply annoying. Sometimes accompanied by blood in the stool, hemorrhoids are normally not cause for concern but can require surgery in severe cases. The recommendations for treatment of hemorrhoids range from topical creams to ingested digestion aids that can combine to alleviate the condition by curing the cause and treating the resulting symptoms. If you're seeking natural alternatives to the chemical-laden, over-the-counter options that can cause constipation and diarrhea or further agitate the affected area, try apple cider vinegar.

Apple cider vinegar has long been used as an effective treatment for hemorrhoids and is reported to provide relief from the inside out that far surpasses the over-the-counter alternatives. Acting as digestive aids that assist in moving waste through the digestive system more efficiently, the pectin, acetic acid, and malic acid contained in ACV combine to bind with waste and lubricate the stools as they pass through the bowels, requiring less strain on the bowels during defecation and reducing the incidence of hemorrhoids.

TO MAKE A DRINK TO RELIEVE HEMORRHOIDS, COMBINE:

1 cup water

1 tablespoon ACV

Drink three times daily. You can begin to experience the relief provided by this helpful combination within as little as an hour.

FOR TOPICAL RELIEF, COMBINE:

⅛ cup water

⅛ cup ACV

Soak a cotton ball or soft towel in the mixture, and apply the mixture directly to the affected area as often as needed, reducing inflammation and relieving the pain that results.

67 Soothe Diaper Rash

The term "diaper rash" is most commonly used to refer to the irritation on a baby's backside, resulting from moist conditions that are ever-present in wet or soiled diapers. The same factors that contribute to diaper rash on a baby's bottom can apply to an adult of any age and lead to the same uncomfortable condition. Adults can get "diaper rash" from:

- Debris left behind after wiping the genitals and anus after using the bathroom
- Wearing tight-fitting clothes that make it difficult for the nether regions to "breathe"

Making it difficult to walk, sit, stand, or wear particular types of clothing, diaper rash can interfere with the daily life of babies and adults alike. While many creams and powders promise relief of the condition, ACV not only soothes symptoms, but it also helps to repair and restore the skin's health. Containing vitamins, minerals, and antioxidants that assist in the regeneration of skin cells, ACV also provides antiseptic, antibacterial, antifungal, and antiviral properties that help to keep the skin free of irritants and infection-causing stimuli.

TO MAKE A TOPICAL TREATMENT, COMBINE:

⅓ cup ACV

½ cup water

Soak a cotton ball or soft towel in the solution and apply to the affected area gently every 15 minutes over the course of 2 hours.

68 Mitigate Jellyfish Stings

Few people know much about jellyfish stings or why they can be so painful. Jellyfish release nematocysts from their tentacles, which stick in the skin and release toxins into the blood stream. These nematocysts can cause minor to excruciating pain, and can warrant medical attention in severe cases when breathing and vision are affected. In the less extreme, yet still painful, cases of jellyfish stings, the most well-known treatment is to apply urine to the affected area. While some cases may find the application of urine effective in calming the irritation that results from jellyfish stings, ACV is a natural alternative to urine that can soothe the skin by releasing the tentacles and delivering necessary nutrients to the skin for quick repair.

Apple cider vinegar has acetic acid that acts to soothe jellyfish stings in two ways:

1. Reducing inflammation, allowing the tentacles to release from the skin and stopping the delivery of the toxins to the sufferer's blood stream

2. Neutralizing the reaction within the skin, blood stream, and nerves, relieving the pain of the sting quickly and effectively.

To make a topical solution, apply undiluted ACV directly to the site of a jellyfish sting. Reapply as needed.

WHILE YOU'RE STILL EXPERIENCING PAIN, MAKE A DRINK BY COMBINING:

1 tablespoon ACV

1 cup water

Drink once an hour for 4 hours to alleviate inflammation, deliver essential reparative vitamins and minerals to the skin, and assist in removing the toxins from the blood stream and organs.

69 Relieve Insect Bites

Being bitten or stung by an insect can set off a series of reactions that can range from mildly uncomfortable to life-threatening. While most insect stings and bites are not life-threatening, they can create skin conditions that itch, burn, or sting, and can last for hours, days, or even weeks! Use apple cider vinegar as a healing treatment for bites you have—and even to avoid future bites!

The naturally occurring acids and enzymes in apple cider vinegar act as a deterrent against bugs that can bite and sting. Able to detect the distasteful and aromatic elements of ACV from afar, bugs are discouraged from even approaching an individual that has ACV on the skin.

TO MAKE A BUG SPRAY, COMBINE IN A SPRAY BOTTLE:

1 cup ACV

¼ cup water

Spray the skin with the mixture or use a towel to apply the solution to the skin and effectively deter bugs from stinging or biting.

To make a topical treatment for soothing stings and bites, apply undiluted ACV to the skin with a towel or cotton ball every 15 minutes. Not only does this prevent inflammation at the site of the sting or bite; it also helps to neutralize the venom excreted by the insect.

Do not hesitate to seek immediate medical attention if you think your particular reaction warrants medical intervention.

70 Manage Nail Fungus

Did you know that apple cider vinegar acts as an effective treatment for fungus, as well as bacteria, viruses, and germs? Able to be taken orally or applied externally in order to treat and prevent fungal infections of the nails, ACV has unique uses and benefits that far outweigh those of prescriptions and over-the-counter medications. ACV naturally delivers:

- Antifungal agents along with a variety of immunity-boosting vitamins
- Minerals that assist in the reparation and healthy growth of nails
- Antioxidants that help to support the prevention of future fungal growth

TO MAKE A DRINK, COMBINE:

1 cup water

1 tablespoon ACV

Drink two or three times daily for use as both a treatment and preventive measure.

ACV has also proven to be effective in killing fungus and restoring nail health when applied directly to the site of fungal growth. The ACV seeps under the nail, penetrating through the nails' pores, and treats the surrounding nail bed.

TO MAKE A NAIL SOAK, POUR UNDILUTED ACV INTO A SMALL BOWL.

Let the nails rest there for 15–30 minutes at a time every other hour until the fungus subsides.

71 Treat Calluses and Corns

Rough, raised skin conditions such as calluses and corns result from pressure and friction on certain areas of the feet that are most often exposed to excessive or prolonged rubbing in shoes, creating a deposit of skin cells in the affected areas. While abrasive treatments such as pumice stones are commonly used to effectively grind down hardened skin deposits, many sufferers of this condition can instead use apple cider vinegar as an effective treatment. With ample amounts of powerful vitamins, minerals, acids, and enzymes, apple cider vinegar helps to prevent the growth of calluses and corns while reducing the size of the existing skin conditions and relieving the pain associated with them.

Use ACV topically to help improve blood flow, soften the skin, and regenerate skin cells.

TO MAKE A TOPICAL TREATMENT, COMBINE IN A TUB OR BUCKET:

1 cup ACV

1 warmed gallon of water

Soak for 30 minutes, 3–5 times daily.

In addition to the benefits that an ACV soak provides (softening the skin, improved circulation, reducing inflammation, and removing dead skin cells), ACV soaks help to prevent the future development of calluses and corns by keeping skin from hardening and accruing more dead skin cells that result in the unsightly condition.

72 Relieve Burns

Surprisingly, apple cider vinegar has long been used as a first-aid treatment for minor burns. Because of its acidity, most people are surprised at the suggestion of using ACV as a burn treatment, assuming the acids would aggravate the burn or cause additional pain. Quite the contrary, apple cider vinegar has potent properties that assist in relieving the pain of a burn, soothing the site of irritation, and delivering nutrients that assist in the healing process while also safeguarding the burn sufferer from infection. The naturally occurring enzymes, acids, and vitamins and minerals of ACV synergistically help to:

- Reduce inflammation
- Speed the healing process
- Prevent germs, bacteria, and viruses from entering the body through the wound
- Promote reparative skin cell production

Whether your burn is the result of hot liquids or chemicals coming into contact with your skin, first treat the affected area with a cool compress or a cool soak to return the affected area's temperature to normal. Then, proceed with an ACV soak.

TO MAKE AN ACV SOAK, COMBINE:

2 cups water

½ cup ACV

Submerge the affected area for 15 minutes at a time over the course of 2–3 hours.

This combination has shown to be an effective method of treatment that can be used for days following the burn, helping to soothe a burn site and jump-start the healing process. Following the soaking treatments, you can also utilize the many components of ACV to reduce the pain and inflammation at the site of the burn.

TO MAKE A BANDAGE AID, COMBINE:

2 cups water

½ cup ACV

Soak the gauze in the ACV mixture and wrap the wound loosely. This process continues the delivery of healing components to the site of the burn.

73 Heal Bruises

A bruise is the visible result of subcutaneous blood vessels being broken, and it can be accompanied with sensitivity or pain in the affected area. Because few topical treatments are suggested for treating bruises, most people adopt a "wait it out" mentality and allow the bruise to heal on its own. However, there are ways to speed the healing process of a bruise and reduce the unsightly appearance of the red, purple, green, or black in the area. One such method is a double dose of apple cider vinegar that can be taken orally and also applied to the site of the bruise, helping to speed the healing process and reduce the inflammation and discoloration that results.

ACV helps bruises by:

- Delivering acids and enzymes that assist the blood in its cleansing process and help the body to detoxify the blood of waste products such as the broken blood vessels

- Supplying vitamin C and beta carotene to support the immune system's functioning, fight infection that could result from the trauma that caused the bruise, and help to repair and regenerate valuable blood cells

TO MAKE A HEALING DRINK, COMBINE:

1 cup water

1 tablespoon ACV

Drink once daily as symptoms persist.

TO MAKE A TOPICAL TREATMENT FOR BRUISES, COMBINE:

¼ cup water

¼ cup ACV

Soak a washcloth in the mixture and apply directly to the site of the bruise, helping to improve blood flow and circulation and assisting in the healing process.

74 Reduce the Appearance of Facial "Masks"

Using a combination of apple cider vinegar and other health-restoring items as a topical facial mask has shown to alleviate symptoms of skin irritation like redness, acne, and discoloration while improving the appearance and quality of the skin. Helping to balance the natural oil production of the skin on the face and neck, apple cider vinegar's acetic and malic acids assist in unclogging pores and removing grime that can be deposited on the face throughout everyday life. Helping to restore a beneficial pH balance to the skin, ACV has shown drastic results in acne sufferers' reduction of irritation and incidence of pimples and blemishes on the skin. (For more, see entry 80, Get Rid of Acne.) Rich in vitamin C and beta carotene, ACV's most impressive benefit is the reduction in free radical damage to the skin on a cellular level, improving the health of the skin and preventing further skin damage that can result from exposure to everyday toxins like smoke, UV light, and air pollution.

TO MAKE A BENEFICIAL SKIN MASK, MASH THE FOLLOWING INGREDIENTS INTO A PASTE:

½ cup ACV

½ of 1 avocado

1 tablespoon natural, unprocessed, organic honey

Apply directly to the skin for 15–30 minutes, removing the mask by rinsing with warm water.

This specific combination of foods contains rich amounts of antioxidants, healthy fats, vitamins, minerals, and enzymes that absorb into the skin and help to:

- Promote blood flow
- Repair damage
- Restore skin health
- Regulate pH and oil production
- Remove dirt and germs from the skin's surface and pores

75 Fade Sunspots

Sunspots appear on the skin in round white patches that may or may not be rough or slightly raised. Long thought to be the result of extensive sun exposure, sunspots are most effectively prevented by reducing the exposure of the skin to the sun's UV rays, wearing clothing to block sunlight from sensitive areas of the skin, and using creams and ointments that prevent sunspots from occurring. While sunlight does aggravate the skin and produce an environment in which sunspots can appear, many medical professionals recommend that sunspot sufferers treat the condition as a fungal infection. For preventive measures, promoting skin cell health and regeneration, and effective antifungal treatments, look no further than apple cider vinegar as an all-encompassing treatment.

The vitamin C present in ACV acts to promote skin health by acting as a powerful antioxidant that can protect skin cells from damage and changes, while also reducing the instance of discoloration on the skin's surface. You can introduce those benefits to your body through this simple drink.

TO MAKE A DRINK, COMBINE:

1 cup water or coconut milk

1 tablespoon ACV

1 teaspoon organic honey

Drink daily.

Because of its antifungal properties, ACV has also shown to be effective as a topical treatment for sunspots.

TO MAKE A TOPICAL TREATMENT, COMBINE:

¼ cup water

¼ cup ACV

Soak a cotton ball or towel in the mixture and apply directly to the skin for 30 minutes. Repeat this process until the appearance of the sunspots has faded completely.

76 Lessen Age Spots

Age spots are brown or tan oval-shaped discolorations on the skin that result from exposure to the sun over long periods of time. These hyperpigmented reactions normally develop in men and women over the age of forty and can become darker and more noticeable as time goes on. While there are chemical treatments and laser treatments designed to whiten these areas and better blend them with surrounding skin tones, many age spot sufferers choose to improve the appearance of their skin through more natural methods such as apple cider vinegar.

With ample amounts of vitamin C and beta carotene that act as powerful antioxidants, apple cider vinegar can assist in the repair of damaged skin cells. In addition to repairing the skin's cells, ACV also acts to regenerate the skin cells and improve the appearance of age spots by renewing the skin's surface.

TO MAKE A TOPICAL AID, COMBINE:

¼ cup ACV

¼ cup water

Apply to the age spots directly on a towelette for 30 minutes three times per day.

Many have reported seeing dramatic improvements in the appearance of age spots after a few short weeks of this treatment. In addition, you can also aid the body's reparative systems in regenerating skin cells and fighting free radical damage by consuming a daily ACV drink.

TO MAKE A DRINK, COMBINE:

1 cup water

1 tablespoon ACV

Drink daily.

77 Counteract Varicose Veins

Varicose veins are those bulging or discolored veins that can be accompanied by pain and sensitivity or simply be an eyesore. Caused by pressure and a reduction in circulation to the affected area, varicose veins are most commonly in the legs, feet, and ankles. Some contributing factors to varicose veins are tight-fitting clothing, extended periods of standing or walking, and crossing the legs at the knee while sitting. In order to reduce the chances of developing varicose veins, you can:

- Wear less-restrictive clothing
- Improve your diet and remain hydrated
- Rub your feet and legs to improve circulation
- Prop up your feet while sitting to reduce the pressure placed on the lower extremities

Another treatment that has shown to be quite helpful in alleviating varicose veins is apple cider vinegar. With blood-improving qualities that help to detoxify and increase circulation, ACV can prevent circumstances that may aggravate the veins in the legs, ankles, and feet while also helping to remove dead cells and blood vessels from the affected areas.

TO MAKE A DRINK, COMBINE IN A BLENDER:

1 cup coconut milk

1 cup strawberries (or kiwi or other tropical fruit)

1 tablespoon ACV

Ice, as needed

Blend until desired consistency is achieved, and drink daily.

TO MAKE A TOPICAL TREATMENT, COMBINE:

¼ cup water

¼ cup ACV

Soak a towel or washcloth with the mixture and apply directly to veins for 20–30 minutes at a time. This topical treatment helps to reduce inflammation of the skin and veins while also promoting circulation and blood flow on-site.

78 Cleanse and Stave Off Infection from Cuts

The most dangerous result of a cut or abrasion is infection. Once the skin has been opened, irritants like germs, bacteria, viruses, and fungi are able to seep into the blood stream and cause infection at the site of the cut, as well as throughout the body. Cleaning the cut thoroughly with warm water and soap and covering the wound with a bandage are the two most important and efficient preventive measures you can take to minimize the risk of infection. The most beneficial steps to take to safeguard your health and the wound itself are to ensure that:

1. The wound remains free of foreign toxins

2. Your immune system is functioning properly

Apple cider vinegar is able to provide both of these health-boosting benefits.

Packed with antiseptic, antiviral, and antibacterial properties, apple cider vinegar can help fight any immune system assailants that are present, as well as safeguard the wound from any future germ exposure. ACV also contains powerful antioxidants that can assist in the regeneration of skin cells, improving the recovery process.

TO MAKE A TOPICAL SOLUTION, COMBINE:

1 tablespoon water

1 tablespoon ACV

Following the cleansing and prior to covering the wound, apply to the wound in order to provide additional protection against infection and improve the natural healing process.

You can also drink ACV to optimize your immune system functioning and safeguard your health from germs that enter the site of the cut and travel through the blood stream. Fighting free radicals and toxins in the blood, ACV has powerful vitamins, minerals, and nutrients that combine to effectively combat immune system attackers, leaving your body healthy and able to heal properly.

TO MAKE THE DRINK, COMBINE:

1 cup water

1 tablespoon ACV

Drink daily while the cut is still healing.

79 Make Your Own Deodorant

Odor on the body can be caused by a number of factors that range from sweat to bacteria, and it is most often strongest in areas of the body that are restricted by clothing or creased, allowing moisture to settle (such as the armpits) where bacteria can thrive. An alarming number of people are unaware that they're placing chemical-laden, store-bought deodorants directly onto a thin layer of skin that covers lymph nodes and veins in the armpit. This highway of blood-transporting veins and nodes absorbs the chemicals and additives in deodorants and antiperspirants and delivers them throughout the body in the blood stream. Because of the possibility of health hazards that can result from the chemicals used in these products, many consumers are opting for natural forms of deodorants that safely and effectively kill the cause of the odor without risking their health.

Apple cider vinegar can be used as an effective deodorant that does not pose health risks and actually boosts the body's overall health.

TO MAKE A HOMEMADE DEODORANT, COMBINE:

1   tablespoon water

1   tablespoon ACV

Apply the mixture to the armpit or area of odor with a cotton ball and allow to dry.

Not only does this application kill odor-causing and infection-breeding bacteria; it is absorbed into the blood stream and helps to assist the body's everyday functioning by ensuring the systems throughout the body receive necessary nutrients.

TO MAKE A PREVENTIVE DRINK, COMBINE:

1   cup water

1   tablespoon ACV

Drink daily to reap the benefits of health-boosting vitamins, minerals, and antioxidants that prevent odor-causing bacteria from breeding within the body and on the skin's surface.

80 Get Rid of Acne

Acne sufferers have long searched for the resolution of blemishes that can appear on the face, neck, chest, back, and arms. Prescription medications and over-the-counter treatments are sometimes expensive, ineffective, or loaded with harsh chemicals and additives. In order to treat the condition safely, naturally, and effectively, acne sufferers can use apple cider vinegar in a number of ways. Apple cider vinegar can be used in four effective treatment options (as a soak, tonic, topical treatment, or facial mask) that are inexpensive, easy to use, and completely risk-free!

The treatments that include apple cider vinegar, when applied directly to the skin in a soak/bath, facial cleanser, or mask, are intended to achieve a number of regulatory and restorative balances in the skin that will help to alleviate the causes of acne and prevent future occurrences. When applied directly to the skin, apple cider vinegar's antioxidants, vitamins, minerals, acids, and enzymes work synergistically to:

- Restore a normal pH to the skin
- Regulate oil production that can lead to the clogging of pores
- Reduce inflammation at the site of blemishes
- Improve circulation in the skin to reduce the appearance of blemishes and redness that so often accompany acne

TO MAKE A SOAK, COMBINE:

Tub full of water

2–4 cups ACV

Soak for up to 30 minutes.

TO MAKE A TONIC, COMBINE:

1 cup water

1 tablespoon ACV

Drink daily.

TO MAKE A TOPICAL TREATMENT, COMBINE:

¼ cup ACV

⅛ cup water

Apply to skin as needed.

TO MAKE A FACIAL MASK, COMBINE:

½ mashed avocado

¼ cup ACV

Apply evenly to face, allowing to set for 10 minutes daily.

Chapter 4: HAIR

Do you spend countless hours and dollars on your regular hair regimen? Do you find yourself dealing with unmanageable locks that lack the volume, shine, or length you dream of? Are you finding it harder and harder to maintain your hair's natural beauty? Or are you simply tired of wasting money on chemical-laden hair-care products that promise the world but fail to deliver? If you consider how many hair products you use on a daily basis, between shampooing and styling, you can imagine how much residue from those products gets left behind. All of that residue and buildup from the products that are intended to help your hair result actually hinder natural growth, shine, body, highlights, and so much more! Because of the damage this buildup can cause to your hair's follicles, cuticles, pores, and ends, you can be left with an unmanageable head of hair that is so unhealthy no product could help! Look no further: apple cider vinegar will restore natural health to your hair and help you attain the hair you've always dreamed of!

ACV contains an astounding variety of naturally occurring acids, enzymes, vitamins, and minerals that work synergistically to deliver nutrition healthy hair requires, can be used in different formulations to act as everything from a clarifying rinse and shampoo to an effective preparation for more vibrant and longer-lasting color-treatments, and is safe enough to drink.

Supported with scientific explanations of how and why this product and the combinations and treatments for each specific benefit work to eliminate the hair issues you deal with daily, these easy-to-create and simple-to-use treatments can quickly provide the results you want while repairing the damage that your hair "care" products have done.

The bottom line is this: If you want to achieve the results you have dreamt of for ages, are tired of spending time and money on products and treatments that are not delivering, and want to use an all-natural product, try apple cider vinegar. Start repairing your hair and get on your way to the beautiful hair you imagine by implementing these ACV treatments today!

81 Help Thinning Hair

Thinning hair can be an embarrassing condition, and it doesn't only strike older men. Women of all ages are becoming a large part of the consumer pool looking for remedies to prevent thinning hair. While prescription drugs and over-the-counter medications promise to deliver powerful results, they often contain harsh chemicals and additives that can pose health risks and aggravate certain medical conditions. If you're looking to reap the benefits of thinning hair treatments safely and effectively with natural products, look no further than a trusty bottle of apple cider vinegar.

By applying apple cider vinegar directly to the site of thinning hair, you can:

- Improve the blood circulation of the scalp
- Improve the blood flow to hair follicles
- Ensure effective delivery of essential nutrients to the scalp

These health-boosting benefits provided by ACV help to promote hair growth and prevent hair loss. ACV also contains valuable vitamins, minerals, and proteins that provide the skin with essential nutrients needed to produce healthy hair and maintain quality proteins within the hair shaft.

TO MAKE A HAIR TONIC, COMBINE:

2 tablespoons ACV

1 tablespoon water

½ teaspoon cayenne pepper

Apply directly to the site of thinning hair, rubbing the mixture into the scalp for 5 minutes. Allow it to sit on the scalp for 1 hour before shampooing as usual. You can start to see results within 2–4 weeks.

Two chemical compounds in cayenne, capsaicin and quercetin, are the beneficial components that help stimulate hair growth by stimulating hair follicles and improving blood flow of the scalp.

82 Beat Dandruff

Dandruff can be caused by a number of factors, but is most likely due to:

- Chemicals within certain hair-care products
- Specific types of bacteria that affect the scalp
- Toxic elements in the environment

Regardless of the cause, apple cider vinegar is able to restore the natural pH balance to the scalp, moisturize the skin, and return the hair condition to one without dry, flaky, or irritating residue.

ACV provides essential acids that act to return the scalp's pH to a normal, healthy level, which is also beneficial to the balance of oils needed to maintain moisture without an overly oily residue. ACV is also able to provide relief to the scalp by reducing inflammation, improving circulation beneath the skin of the scalp, and delivering essential nutrients directly to the sites affected.

TO MAKE A SCALP-SOOTHING SOLUTION, COMBINE:

½ cup ACV

1 cup warmed liquid coconut oil

Apply the mixture to the scalp, and allow to sit on the scalp for 30–45 minutes. Rinse before shampooing and conditioning as normal.

You can also follow up the ACV and coconut oil treatment with this scalp rinse.

TO MAKE A SCALP RINSE, COMBINE:

⅓ cup ACV

1 cup warm water

Rinse the scalp with the solution after shampooing and conditioning, before towel-drying hair.

83 Make Your Own Hair Rinse

While most hair-care products effectively provide what they promise, many leave unsightly residue and buildup on the hair follicles, hair shafts, and scalp. This buildup can lead to excessively oily hair, unmanageable frizz, or lackluster color. Comically, many hair products promise to remove this residue by using chemicals and harsh abrasives that can lead to hair that is dry and unmanageable, meaning you traded one problem for another. By using apple cider vinegar as a rinse following the normal shampooing and conditioning treatments, you can effectively remove residue and restore your hair's health, shine, and color naturally and without adverse side effects.

With acids and enzymes that cleanse, and vitamins and minerals that nourish, apple cider vinegar can clear the hair of debris and buildup without damaging the hair's follicles or disrupting the scalp's pH balance.

TO MAKE A HAIR RINSE, COMBINE:

1 cup water

½ cup ACV

Apply it to the hair following your regular routine of shampooing and conditioning. Allow the mixture to sit on the hair and scalp for 5 minutes before rinsing with warm water. Repeating this procedure with every other wash will ensure your hair stays free of buildup that weighs down hair.

84 Make Your Own Shampoo

Some shampoos leave you with luscious locks that bounce, shine, and stay frizz-free, while others leave your hair feeling weighed down, dried out, or full of frizz. Trying out different brands can be costly, time-consuming, and damaging to your hair. By using apple cider vinegar as a shampoo alternative, you can naturally cleanse the hair and add beauty and health to your strands. You might even see and feel an improvement in the quality of your hair after just one treatment! ACV is inexpensive, natural, and doesn't contain harsh chemicals and additions (which can actually increase the frequency of bad hair days). ACV will supply your hair with these amazing benefits:

- Cleanse your hair of grime and buildup
- Add health-fortifying vitamins and minerals directly to the hair and scalp for improved shine, volume, and bounce
- Provide everything from restorative proteins to pH-neutralizing enzymes
- Promote hair health and restore beauty to strands
- Gently remove environmental deposits

TO MAKE SHAMPOO, COMBINE IN A BOTTLE:

½ cup ACV

2 tablespoons lemon juice

1 cup water

Use the mixture in place of your shampoo, massaging it into the scalp and strands, rinsing, and proceeding to condition as you routinely would. You can use this shampoo substitute every wash, or use it alternately with your regular shampoo.

85 Make Your Own Conditioner

Nowadays, you can find deep conditioning treatments at home and in the salon, as well as balms and solutions that promise to leave hair silky and hydrated. The variety of conditioning treatments is dizzying. Depending upon whether your hair is oily, dry, curly, or straight, different conditioners designed to treat all hair types may fall flat on delivering their promised results. Surprisingly enough, the same bottle of apple cider vinegar you use for your daily tonics that keep you healthy and energized can also work wonders as a conditioner for hair of all types, shades, and textures. A number of treatment options may be available, but few provide the nutrients contained in ACV, are as inexpensive as ACV, and provide results after the very first treatment like ACV does!

Combined with the additional conditioning components of coconut oil, ACV is an effective conditioner that tames frizz, fights tangles, and keeps locks lustrous while improving the pH levels of the scalp and closing the hair follicles.

TO MAKE CONDITIONER, COMBINE IN A BOTTLE:

½ cup ACV

¼ cup liquid coconut oil

1 cup water

Apply the treatment to your hair, cover hair with a shower cap, and allow the mixture to set for 30 minutes. Then rinse and dry, revealing renewed hair with restored health.

86 Combat Baldness

Baldness can occur as a result of genetics, repeated damaging hair treatments, or lack of sufficient dietary elements that support the health and growth of hair. In its unfiltered state, ACV contains a number of helpful enzymes, proteins, vitamins, minerals, and naturally occurring acids that combine to:

- Contribute cleansing and restorative elements directly to the site of baldness
- Remove agitating causes that can contribute to baldness
- Improve the conditions of the hair and scalp, promoting new hair growth and maintaining the health of that hair growth

Chemical-laden hair-regenerating products can actually irritate the scalp, damage the hair, and interfere with the absorption and utilization of essential elements needed for healthy hair growth. Instead, use only natural-ingredient shampoos, conditioners, and treatments such as ACV. Finally, in an effort to spot-treat baldness and internally balance key physical nutrients, you can use two effective treatments: a topical ACV treatment and an ingested ACV tonic.

TO MAKE A TONIC, COMBINE:

½ cup water

½ cup ACV

½ teaspoon cayenne pepper

Apply the mixture directly to the scalp at the areas where baldness is appearing. Leave the mixture on the scalp for a period of 30 minutes, then shampoo and condition as normal. Following this routine on a daily basis has shown to improve baldness in 2–4 weeks!

TO MAKE A DRINKABLE TONIC, COMBINE:

1 cup water

1 tablespoon ACV

Drink daily.

This drink provides the dietary components in ACV such as the vitamins, minerals, enzymes, and acids that:

- Support the health of systems directly related to the growth and health of hair, such as metabolism and blood flow
- Help resolve deficiencies that can contribute to baldness, such as some B vitamins, vitamin C, vitamin D, and iron

87 Improve Hair Porosity

"Porosity" is the term that refers to the hair's ability to absorb and retain moisture. Low-porosity hair is able to absorb and retain moisture well, while high-porosity hair does not. The strands of your hair contain pores and hair shafts that allow moisture into the hair when wet. When you are suffering from dry, oily, frizzy, or unmanageable hair, it is most commonly due to damage to the hair's cuticle and pores, complicating the process of the hair's ability to obtain and/or retain moisture. The hair's cuticle is the outer layer of the hair that looks very similar to shingles on a roof, and when grime from the environment or a number of styling products and processes settle on the hair's cuticles, it can result in clogged pores that don't allow moisture to be absorbed. The hair's pores can also be affected by styling processes that damage the cuticle. As a result, the pores do not open to allow moisture in; nor do they close tightly (which is what allows the hair to appear shiny and sleek, without frizz). When these normal processes are troubled by damaging products and treatments, the effective corrective treatment has to focus on restoring the natural health to the hair's porosity. For an effective, natural solution for high-porosity hair, you can use apple cider vinegar.

By combining natural ingredients that contain protein, fats, and vitamins and minerals, you can deliver essential elements to your hair that restore hair health quickly, easily, and naturally!

TO MAKE A HAIR-CARE SOLUTION, COMBINE IN A BLENDER AT ROOM TEMPERATURE:

½ cup ACV

½ cup almond milk

¼ cup liquid coconut oil

2 tablespoons honey

Apply to the hair. Once the hair is soaked with the ACV treatment, put on a shower cap, and leave on for 30 minutes before rinsing. Performing this treatment every day or every other day, you will notice a return of healthy shine and texture to your hair in 1–2 weeks.

88 Detangle Hair

When your hair is a tangled mess and you have trouble simply brushing or combing it after a shower, you may be inclined to use a detangling product. While many products on the market promise to leave your hair healthy and free of tangles, a large number of them contain chemicals or unnatural substances that can strip healthy elements from hair, leaving your strands lackluster and damaged. In order to fight tangles while retaining the health of hair, try ACV!

Containing restorative and essential vitamins and minerals, ACV can reduce tangles by removing residue and buildup left behind from cleaning products, while also moisturizing and conditioning your strands and making them more manageable and easier to style.

TO MAKE A DETANGLING SPRAY, COMBINE IN A SPRAY BOTTLE:

½ cup ACV

1 cup water

Spray your hair with the ACV solution from the scalp to the ends of your hair, combing through locks and relieving tangles. There's no need to rinse the solution, so you can simply style your hair as you normally would and enjoy the added benefits of shine and manageability, too!

89 Reduce Frizz

Frizzy hair is a frustrating condition that can be caused by the weather or extensive exposure to damaging elements contained in hair products and hair treatments. The crux of frizzy hair issues is high porosity that is caused by the shaft of hair strands remaining open and unable to retain moisture. The drying out of these strands makes them susceptible to effects of the climate or styling products and treatments that lead to hair appearing "frizzy." By delivering naturally restorative proteins and nutrients to your hair strands, you can actually spot-treat frizziness and enjoy healthy, shiny, manageable hair. You might see "natural" products on the market, but be sure you read the ingredients carefully—many are labeled "natural" but they still contain certain preservatives or synthetic materials that can lead to hair damage. In order to avoid unnecessary "bad hair days" caused by frizz, you need to look no further than apple cider vinegar.

ACV contains rich amounts of proteins and enzymes that provide hair with restorative health benefits.

TO MAKE AN IN-SHOWER ANTIFRIZZ TREATMENT, COMBINE IN A BOTTLE:

½ cup ACV

½ cup water

2 teaspoons liquid coconut oil

After conditioning in the shower, apply the mixture to your hair and leave it on for 5 minutes. Then rinse the solution from the hair and dry as you would routinely.

TO MAKE A PRESTYLING, FRIZZ-FIGHTING SOLUTION, COMBINE IN A SPRAY BOTTLE:

1 cup water

½ cup ACV

Saturate damp hair with the ACV spray. After allowing the spray to settle for 5 minutes, towel-dry and style as you would routinely.

90 Prevent Split Ends

Split ends occur when the end of a hair strand breaks into two strands that then proceed to split the hair from the bottom up. Not only does this damage the hair, but it can make the appearance and the maintenance and styling of hair difficult and frustrating. By trimming only the ends of your hair every month, you can prevent split ends before they start and keep healthy hair free of split-end damage. Another way to prevent split ends is to ensure that you have the proper intake of essential vitamins and minerals that contribute to healthy hair growth, like silica, calcium, vitamin C, and B vitamins. A plentiful vitamin and mineral intake will improve your hair's health from the inside out and prevent split ends from occurring. To treat split ends most effectively, you can use all-natural, unfiltered, organic apple cider vinegar as an ingested preventive measure as well as a topical remedy, providing relief from split ends forever!

TO MAKE A DRINK THAT ENSURES YOUR VITAMIN AND MINERAL INTAKE IS OPTIMAL, COMBINE:

1 cup water

1 tablespoon ACV

Drink daily.

TO MAKE A TOPICAL TREATMENT FOR SPLIT ENDS, COMBINE:

½ cup water

½ cup ACV

¼ cup mashed avocado

Rub the mixture into the bottom ¼ of hair, and allow to set for 30 minutes before rinsing thoroughly. Repeat this treatment two or three times weekly, and you can effectively prevent split ends, seeing results in a matter of a few short weeks.

91 Kill and Prevent Head Lice

Head lice can be an embarrassing and frustrating issue, especially considering that the most commonly affected population is school-aged children. In close quarters like classrooms with large numbers of children, head lice are easily transferred from person to person. Limiting exposure to anyone with confirmed head lice is the first preventive measure that can effectively reduce the chance of contracting head lice. If you find yourself dealing with a confirmed case of head lice, though, you must not only treat the head lice, but also take precautionary measures to ensure the lice die and have no chance of returning to cause the condition again.

Many drugstore products are available that can treat head lice, but most contain chemicals and synthetic additives that can be hazardous to your health or dangerous to adults and children with specific skin sensitivities. As a natural alternative, try ACV.

TO MAKE A HEAD LICE TREATMENT:

Apply undiluted apple cider vinegar to the hair and scalp, covering the hair with a shower cap. Allow the vinegar to remain on the hair for at least 4–5 hours. After removing the cap and rinsing the hair with water, carefully comb through the hair with a fine-tooth comb, removing the nits and eggs.

Repeat this process daily until all lice and eggs are gone.

92 Promote Hair Growth

The number of hair-growth products on the market is overwhelmingly large and is increasing every year. The difference between one product and another can be the chemical components, the claims to be "all-natural," or the guarantees that growth will follow the product's use. While the promotions can seem promising, the actual results can vary product to product and person to person depending upon a number of factors. By combining a number of effective hair-growth methods with ACV, you can effectively and inexpensively improve your hair growth naturally.

Apple cider vinegar has long been promoted for a large number of uses that promote health because of its high amounts of essential vitamins and minerals. With natural acids, enzymes, and proteins also contained within every drop of ACV, it is now accepted as an effective ingredient for treating hair loss and supporting hair growth. By massaging the scalp daily, eating a balanced diet high in protein, and minimizing the hair's exposure to heat treatments and harmful chemicals, you can maintain hair health.

TO MAKE A NIGHTLY HAIR GROWTH TREATMENT, COMBINE:

1 cup ACV

1 cup aloe juice

Apply directly to the scalp and throughout the hair to the ends, cover with a shower cap, and sleep with the applied mixture on the hair for 7–8 hours. Shower or rinse your hair in the morning. You can improve the health of your hair, restore natural essential nutrients, and see and feel the results in 2–4 weeks.

93 Add Shine

One of the most common complaints about hair is that it is dull, and hair-care companies know this all too well. To the rescue of lackluster hair, millions of products that promise to return light-reflective shine to your dull mane are available at your favorite grocery store, drugstore, salon, or hair product website and can range in price from $1 to over $100! If you're hoping to remedy your lackluster locks and return the beautiful glow we associate with healthy hair, you needn't look any further than your trusty bottle of apple cider vinegar.

By introducing apple cider vinegar into your diet and hair treatment routine, you can:

- Restore the natural balance of nutrients to your body's systems that promote hair health
- Topically improve your hair's condition and appearance by stripping away residue and buildup left behind from styling products
- Repair damage done by heat and chemical treatments intended to style, color, or treat hair

TO MAKE A SHINY-HAIR DRINK, COMBINE:

1 cup water

1 tablespoon ACV

Drink daily to deliver an abundance of vitamins, minerals, acids, and enzymes that assist in maintaining hair health.

TO MAKE A TOPICAL HAIR SOLUTION, COMBINE:

1 cup water

1 cup ACV

2 tablespoons essential oil of peppermint

After shampooing and conditioning, apply the solution to hair and work through strands. Allow the mixture to set for 5–10 minutes before rinsing thoroughly.

This treatment can restore hair health to the shaft, pores, and cuticles of hair strands, helping to repair damage and restore a healthy sheen naturally.

94 Add Highlights

If you're looking for natural at-home methods to highlight your hair that can replace your expensive and hair-damaging salon highlight treatments, you can easily exchange the costly chemical treatments for all-natural ACV to achieve the same beautiful results.

ACV contains a number of acids and enzymes that can help naturally lighten hair strands when exposed to the sun. You just need to combine ACV with other ingredients that assist in the lightening process while also conditioning the treated strands with natural oils.

TO MAKE A HAIR LIGHTENER, COMBINE AT ROOM TEMPERATURE:

1 cup water

½ cup fresh-squeezed lemon juice

¼ cup liquid coconut oil

½ cup ACV

Apply it to the hair, and allow the wet hair to be exposed to direct sunlight for 20–30 minutes. This treatment can improve the appearance of highlights naturally, inexpensively, and effectively in as little as one treatment.

95 Protect Against Chlorine Damage

If you've ever seen a pool-loving child in the summertime, you've seen the chlorine aftereffects that can transform the color of any locks to a deep green, dry out the hair, and turn even the most beautiful head of hair to one of unmanageable frizz and damaged split ends. If you can't resist the pool, and can't bear the thought of chlorine damage, what's a protective treatment that you can use? What treatment option can reverse chlorine damage as well as prevent it? What treatment option is inexpensive, requires no visits to the salon, and can be used daily without damaging hair? Apple cider vinegar.

With natural compounds that close the hair shaft correctly, protecting the hair strands from chemical damage such as chlorine damage, apple cider vinegar creates a perfect environment for hair to block infiltrating chemicals that can destroy hair quality from the inside out. Containing natural components that strip away grime, buildup, and excess chemical residue, apple cider vinegar can also be used as an effective rinse that can rid even the blondest of hair of the green chlorine sheen.

TO MAKE A CHLORINE-BUSTING RINSE, COMBINE IN A SPRAY BOTTLE:

1 cup water

2 cups ACV

Apply the mixture before and after exposing hair to chlorine by saturating the hair with the solution and shampooing and rinsing it as you would routinely.

96 Promote Scalp Health

ACV is an alternative to expensive, synthetic products that may or may not work to make your scalp healthier. It's a quick and inexpensive, all-natural, nutrient-rich option, whether your issue with scalp health is mild or severe.

The health of your scalp directly affects the quality of your day. If that sounds a bit extreme, speak to someone who suffers from severe dandruff, bouts of baldness or hair loss, or frequent itchy scalp, and you'll find that scalp health is serious business. By walking into any hair-care aisle of almost any store, you can see that scalp health is also a lucrative business, with thousands of products designed to restore health to your scalp . . . for a price. Whether you pay that price in the expense of the product, or by suffering from health conditions that can be aggravated or a direct result of the chemicals or synthetic ingredients contained in the product, many of the scalp-restorative products don't live up to their promises or are far more than you bargained for.

TO RESTORE HEALTH TO YOUR SCALP, COMBINE:

1 cup water

½ cup ACV

1 teaspoon cayenne pepper

1 teaspoon organic honey

Wet hair and apply mixture to scalp, rubbing into scalp thoroughly. Allow mixture to set on hair and scalp for 30 minutes before rinsing, shampooing, and conditioning as usual. Repeat daily or weekly.

97 Remove Product Residue

Do you use shampoo, conditioner, straightening products, keratin products, curling agents, gel, hairspray, mousse, or leave-in conditioner, or have regular treatments to your hair intended to color or style your locks? If you're one of the billions of consumers who answered yes, you probably have considerable product residue on your hair. While you may not notice by simply looking at or touching your hair, the styling products and treatments you use to cleanse, condition, or treat your hair can leave behind a film of chemical buildup or residue . . . even after washing. If you're one of the millions of people who use clarifying products that promise to rid your hair of this unhealthy buildup, you may be surprised to learn that most of them only partially solve the problem, and many can actually leave behind additional residue.

Turn to ACV to truly cleanse your hair without harsh chemicals or additives that can strip nutrients along with buildup. Clarifying enzymes and acids that naturally occur in apple cider vinegar are the potent contents that make its use as a clarifying product effective, yet safe. In this suggested treatment of two different applications of ACV to your hair, you can quickly and easily remove the buildup of residue left behind by hair products and follow up with a restorative nutrient-rich application that will leave your hair healthier than ever.

TO MAKE A SOAK, COMBINE:

1 cup ACV

½ cup water

Soak your hair from scalp to ends with the solution and cover hair with a shower cap, allowing the mixture to set on your hair for 30 minutes. Rinsing with only water, you can shower as usual, but apply no products to the hair.

TO MAKE A NOURISHING CONDITIONER, COMBINE:

1 cup ACV

½ cup liquid coconut oil

½ cup water

Two hours after rinsing the ACV soak from your scalp, apply this mixture directly to your hair and scalp, massaging it in. Allow the solution to set on hair for 30 minutes, then rinse the solution with water. Comb and towel-dry.

98 Restore Proper pH Balance to the Scalp

Did you know that apple cider vinegar and the scalp have the same pH levels? That's right, your scalp is probably in a more acidic state than you ever thought, but it's not a bad thing . . . necessarily. When most itchy, irritating conditions occur at the scalp, it's because of the disruption in pH levels that are supposed to naturally function in a relatively acidic manner. The disruption in pH that can result from a number of factors, ranging from dietary ingredients to hair products to environmental factors, can be remedied with ACV.

Apple cider vinegar contains valuable nutrients that:

- Nourish the skin, which helps in alleviating some of the symptoms of an imbalanced pH such as itchiness, flaking, inflammation, and redness
- Provide relief by curing the crux of the problem—a pH level that is out of whack

TO MAKE A RINSE, COMBINE:

1 cup ACV

1 cup water

Apply to the scalp; you can experience immediate relief of pH imbalance symptoms, like itchiness.

TO MAKE A SOOTHING SOAK, COMBINE:

1 cup ACV

¼ cup water

Apply the solution to the scalp, covering the hair with a shower cap, and allow the solution to soak on the skin for 30 minutes three times per day until symptoms subside. This treatment has shown to be an effective method in returning the scalp's pH to normal levels, alleviating symptoms and preventing further disruptions.

TO MAKE AN INTERNAL TREATMENT TO BE SURE YOU'RE GETTING ALL THE NUTRIENTS YOU NEED TO MAINTAIN PROPER PH LEVELS LONG TERM, COMBINE:

1 cup water

1 tablespoon ACV

Drink daily to prevent possible pH imbalances in the future while also providing your body with a number of added health benefits.

99 Maintain Color-Treated Hair

Color-treated hair is a favorite among many men and women, but unfortunately, the color often doesn't last as long as you'd like. Because of the naturally occurring acids and enzymes in apple cider vinegar, it has long been used to add highlights to hair naturally. Since it lightens hair, ACV has been pushed aside by those who color-treat their hair and intend to retain that color as long as possible. So it may surprise you that ACV can actually help color-treated hair retain color when used as a precoloring treatment. ACV's vitamins, minerals, and proteins help the soon-to-be-treated hair maintain a soft, sleek, and shiny appearance.

ACV also provides the shaft, pores, and cuticles of the hair with the nourishment they need to maintain health, remain sealed, and be better able to resist the damaging effects that sometimes occur following color treatments.

TO MAKE A HAIR TREATMENT, COMBINE:

½ cup ACV

½ cup water

¼ cup liquid coconut oil

Apply to the scalp, covering with a shower cap, and allow the solution to set on the hair for 30 minutes. Rinse with water and towel-dry hair to reveal nutrient-packed, residue-free locks that are better able to absorb and retain color treatments.

(100) Remove Hard Water Residue

The term "hard water" is used to describe water containing minerals from rocks and sediments in the area from which the water was obtained, in the treatment process of the water or between treatment and your home. If you find yourself dealing with discolored, foul-smelling, or hard-to-manage hair that doesn't suds up when you shampoo, hard water may be to blame. The most effective way to correct hard water is to install a treatment pump or filter that can remove the minerals of your water, but these can be expensive and sometimes ineffective.

Regardless of your long-term plan to treat your water, it is important to treat your hair to rid it of the hard water effects as quickly as possible. Over-the-counter treatments for hard water hair can be costly or loaded with chemicals, so opting for a natural treatment like ACV may be your safest and most effective way to achieve your healthy hair again. With acids and enzymes galore, apple cider vinegar is one of the safest and most effective treatments for ridding hair of residue and buildup. When it comes to removing mineral buildup, ACV is just as effective as top-of-the-line products, but can do so easily, safely, and without posing a risk to hair or skin health. Packed with nourishing nutrients that also help to restore essential vitamins and minerals directly into your strands' cuticles, pores, and shafts, apple cider vinegar can also help reverse damage done by mineral deposits on the hair. The best part? The power of ACV's enzymes and acids can actually remove deposits on hair.

TO MAKE A HAIR RINSE, COMBINE:

1 cup ACV

1 cup water

Apply the solution to hair following shampooing and conditioning as usual. Allow the solution to set on hair for 5 minutes before rinsing.

You can also use the shampoo and conditioner recipes included in this book for natural alternatives to shampoos and conditioners that can leave residues behind.

INDEX

Acknowledgments

First and foremost, I would like to thank my beyond-amazing husband, Jimmy, for his unwavering support—not only in writing this book, but by being my partner in researching and implementing anything and everything we can possibly do to improve our health and the health of our children, with the loving goal to live longer, happier lives together. I am truly blessed!

I could not have written this book at all if it wasn't for the help of my mother-in-law, Robin. I am so thankful to have such an amazingly supportive, strong woman as my mother-in-law, and cannot thank her enough for everything she is and does.

I would also like to thank my editor, Lisa Laing, for giving me the opportunity to write this book—and to research these amazing uses of apple cider vinegar that further support my family's use of this wonderful product, and to share these natural remedies with everyone interested in living a more natural lifestyle.

Photo Credits

Shutterstock: © Aedka Studio 44; © Africa Studio 49, 93; © alisalipa 98; © Billion Photos 33; © Es75 90-91; © id-art 135; © istetiana 69; © Ivaylo Ivanov 88-89; © kozirsky 12-13; © Lecic 125; © lidante 67; © Liv friis-larsen 83; © mama_mia 41; © Alexander Mazurkevich 7, 140; © mythja 15; © Anna Shepulova 109; © Goskova Tatiana 21; © tunedin by Westend61 47; © wasanajai 57; © Gayvoronskaya_Yana 117